CLIFFORD & SON

First published in 2014 by
Liberties Press
140 Terenure Road North | Terenure | Dublin 6W
T: +353 (1) 405 5701 | W: libertiespress.com | E: info@libertiespress.com

Trade enquiries to Gill & Macmillan Distribution
Hume Avenue | Park West | Dublin 12
T: +353 (1) 500 9534 | F: +353 (1) 500 9595 | E: sales@gillmacmillan.ie

Distributed in the United Kingdom by
Turnaround Publisher Services
Unit 3 | Olympia Trading Estate | Coburg Road | London N22 6TZ
T: +44 (0) 20 8829 3000 | E: orders@turnaround-uk.com

Distributed in the United States by
IPM | 22841 Quicksilver Dr | Dulles, VA 20166
T: +1 (703) 661-1586 | F: +1 (703) 661-1547 | E: ipmmail@presswarehouse.com

ISBN: 978-1-909718-39-5
2 4 6 8 10 9 7 5 3 1

A CIP record for this title is available from the British Library.

Cover design by Liberties Press
Internal design by Liberties Press

All food photos by Joanne Murphy, except those on
pp 51, 82-83, 85, 162-64, 210-12, 236-37, 239, 244-45, 247

CLIFFORD & SON

NEW IRISH COOKING FROM MICHAEL & PETER CLIFFORD
WITH JOE MCNAMEE

LIBERTIES

CONTENTS

MAINS

DESSERTS

FOREWORD

Marco Pierre White

Let me set the scene. It was the autumn of 1982, in the kitchen of Le Gavroche. Michel and Albert Roux had first opened the doors of this great restaurant in 1967, slightly hesitant about the reaction they might receive in London. 'What will they make of us and of our food?' the French brothers had wondered.

They needn't have worried. Within a few dinners, Le Gavroche was firmly established as a culinary sensation, serving proper French cuisine to Chelsea residents, Hollywood stars and British royalty alike.

Le Gavroche changed the face of the British restaurant world. It was the standard-bearer. It was the first British restaurant to win a Michelin star (in 1974) and two stars (in 1977). It then became the first British restaurant to win three stars (in 1982), with Albert Roux at the helm. It started life in Lower Sloane Street and, in 1982, moved to a new home in Upper Brook Street, Mayfair, where it remains to this day.

In that same year, in that kitchen in Mayfair, I met Michael Clifford. I was close to the start of my career, and we worked together on the kitchen section known as 'Sauce', responsible for the meat dishes.

It was many years ago but Michael left a deep impression on all who met him. He was a gentleman, incredibly polite and great to work with. Hard-working and disciplined, he was a kind and humble soul and truly passionate about food. That passion would be recognised by a much wider audience in due course. When it was time for him to leave Le Gavroche, Michael returned to Ireland, and here he would go on to ensure himself a well-deserved place in the nation's gastronomic history. Perhaps you were lucky enough to eat his food.

His career included overseeing the kitchens at Arbutus Lodge in Cork, White's on the Green in Dublin and the Cashel Palace Hotel in Cashel. At his restaurant in Cork, Clifford's, he was renowned.

In short, Michael Clifford was a massive influence on Irish cuisine. He was also one of the first Irish chefs to champion Clonakilty Blackpudding, not just as a breakfast staple but as an ingredient on the menus of the finest establishments. Along the way, Michael won a Michelin star and wrote two cookbooks.

I was sad to learn of Michael's untimely death in 2006. What a loss, though I will always think fondly of him and our brief time together.

And then I heard from Michael's son Peter, another chef and one who is certainly getting attention. 'I'm writing a cookbook and it'll be dedicated to dad,' he said. Peter and I share a love of food and we are both sons of chefs. We have both followed in our dads' footsteps. Where Michael left off, Peter picks up . . .

This is a book of recipes – half of them by father Michael, the other half by son Peter. Take a look at them and you'll see how Irish food has developed over the past three decades. I am privileged to have known Messrs Clifford and am honoured to write these opening words for this extremely special and charming book.

That's enough talk. By now you'll be feeling peckish, so let's move on to the magnificent food of *Clifford & Son*.

INTRODUCTION

Joe McNamee

Clifford . . .

On the back cover of this book is a picture of a beaming Michael Clifford. The pensive little chap with the serious expression is his fifteen-year-old son, Peter Clifford. It is March of 2006. Young Peter has just won the regional finals of the Tesco Young Chef of the Year competition and is to compete in the finals in May. There is even a TV crew following Peter, one of six teenage subjects of a documentary on the competition.

A few weeks later, Michael Clifford, the Michelin-starred chef/proprietor of Clifford's, in Clonmel, is preparing for evening service. His wife, Deirdre, notices something odd about his demeanour as he heads out to the garden before beginning service to pick a few last-minute herbs, something he always does. She makes to follow him but someone asks her a question, distracting her for a moment. By the time she reaches the garden, Michael is lying on the ground in some distress. It so happens that two consultants from the local hospital are dining that evening at the restaurant, and they immediately take over. Michael is rushed to Clonmel Regional Hospital and, from there, straight to Cork University Hospital. But it is too late. He is returned to the hospital in Clonmel, where he dies the next day, 6 April 2006.

When the members of the TV production company hear of Michael's death, they assume young Peter will no longer participate in the final, but barely a month after his father's passing, the fifteen-year-old not only takes part but wins with ease. 'I did it for my father,' he says. 'It's what he'd have wanted me to do.'

★

When Michael Clifford died at such a comparatively young age, just fifty-two, his family were, naturally, devastated. Fellow professionals in the food world were also shocked and saddened, for they recognised the importance of Clifford's enormous contribution to Irish cuisine.

Declan Ryan: Michael was one of the finest chefs in Ireland. He was extremely talented and innovative, and ran a highly motivated kitchen brigade. When he died, the restaurant business lost one of its true stars.

His passing was noted in the press at the time, but coverage was muted in an era before the current social-media-fuelled frenzy for all things culinary and, anyway, Michael never wanted to become one of those celebrity chefs who transcend skillet and stove to become icons of popular culture.

To Myrtle Allen, the grande dame of Irish food, must go the credit for 'discovering' Irish produce and for introducing the concepts of provenance and terroir to the professional kitchen, but there followed a generation of highly gifted Irish chefs with the ability to bring a rigorous classical training to bear on this ethos. Michael Clifford was at the forefront of this movement and the story of his culinary accomplishments and his contribution to the history of modern Irish cuisine deserves recording and respect of the highest order.

But Michael was also a reserved, even secretive man, so it is hardly a surprise that only a handful are acquainted with the story of his life before he began his professional cooking career, his upbringing in the care of the State and the religious orders, first in an orphanage and then in an industrial school. It is a remarkable tale, at times quite heartbreaking, and part of a far greater canvas, a deeply shameful period in Irish social history that still resonates today with each fresh unfolding, each further revelation adding grim flesh to the very barest bones of a story he never fully shared, not even with his immediate family. But it is also an inspirational story of how a young boy managed a stellar rise from such gloomy circumstances, with the love and support of a remarkable family from a small Irish country town.

★

Michael Peter Clifford was born in Kerry on 29 June 1953, to Catherine 'Kit' Clifford (née Fleming) of Killeentierna Parish (Currow), about five miles east of Farranfore, and James Clifford of Ardfert. The couple lived near Tralee after they married. When Michael was still an infant, Kit was diagnosed with cervical cancer. She was dead within six weeks. Michael's older brother, Timothy, was taken in by his maternal grandparents; young Michael was put into an orphanage in nearby Killarney.

> TIMOTHY CLIFFORD: He was a baby and I was a toddler. After our mother died it had a huge effect on our father. I don't think he coped well with it. I do remember him but we didn't see him. I was maybe six or seven the last time I saw him. We [my grandparents and I] were in touch with Michael all through our early childhood. He'd be let out to spend a week or so with us during the summers. I guess I was conscious of his situation, being in the orphanage. We used to have an aunt from England – Margaret or 'Peg' – who'd come home most years. That was one of her 'duties' or 'missions', as she saw it – to visit him in Killarney. There was talk that another uncle, living quite nearby, would adopt him, but it fell through.

Liam Collins was a solicitor in Clonakilty, County Cork, and his wife Betty was a pharmacist who, once married, had retired, as was then compulsory for all Irish women. She devoted herself to children. She had eight of her own and fostered a further four. Michael Peter Clifford was one of those four.

> HELEN COLLINS: He's always been Michael Peter, from the day he came to us – we have a brother Michael, Mickey. He was nine going on ten and they all came from the orphanage in Killarney, where my mother knew a nun, Sr Aloysius. My mother said she just fell for Michael Peter when she saw him. How could you not? A beautiful, blonde-haired, blue-eyed boy. For the fostering arrangement, he came at Christmas, Easter and summer and had to return for school to Killarney.
>
> We used to just run wild down in Inchedoney. There was nothing there then but us and another family in three holiday houses. My father bought two houses because there was so many of us. He was a solicitor. I never saw a small saucepan in my life but, though we didn't have much, we had more than most. The first day Michael Peter came, he asked my father was the sea at Inchedoney a big lake, because he'd never seen the sea before.
>
> My mother, God bless her, had a baby every year, so she had a whistle. We all had our turns, peeled potatoes, did the chores and then went off. If she wanted to see if we were all alive, there was one absolute rule: you had to show yourself when the whistle was blown; or near meal-times we had to show up at the house.
>
> One of the fostered girls went down to her room on the first day and put on her apron. She thought she was coming to work for us. Mother said to her quietly, 'Put that away, you'll not need that here.' For Michael Peter and the girls, it was just the freedom of it.
>
> LIZ COLLINS: He was like another member of the family. I was about five when he came first. I had memories of running wild in Inchedoney, the cousins, Michael Peter and the other fostered children all sleeping top to tail. Ironically, it was like running an orphanage. He was always part of it. We'd go to Santy and people described us as having a magic car – you'd open the door and nothing but children would pour out. Then he kind of disappeared from us. They told my mother he'd gone from an all-female environment. She knew in her stomach that it was not good.

Michael, having reached the age of twelve, had been transferred from the orphanage in Killarney to St Joseph's Industrial School in Tralee.

> HELEN COLLINS: In Killarney, he was with the girls. Then, at eleven or twelve, he disappeared. My mother went down to collect him and there was no Michael Peter. He'd been moved out of the orphanage as he was nearly twelve, and the nuns felt that boys should no longer be with the girls from that age on. He was shifted to the reform school in Tralee. She went to Tralee to get him but was told she couldn't have him. She wrote to the bishop. He said she couldn't have him because it would be unsettling for

13

Back row, from left to right: Bridget Fleming, Dick Fleming, Mary O'Rourke, unknown nun, Michael David Fleming; middle row: Timothy Clifford, Maureen Fleming, Michael Fleming; front: Michael Clifford

Timothy and Michael Clifford with their aunt Peg and cousin Bridget

Michael with his foster parents

him to be taken out, and unsettling for the other boys. She wanted to go to the cardinal but my father wouldn't let her. She wrote to Michael Peter every month and sent him parcels but we never saw him again until he was sixteen and was released. And when he was released, they handed him all the letters and presents she had sent him. They had held them all back.

She had no idea what was happening to him. She died in 2001 and one of the last things she said was that she never forgave herself for what happened to him. She said, 'I should have broken down the door and got him.' My mother went to her death broken-hearted for what happened to him, and I couldn't console her about that. They were bad times.

Liz Collins: On her deathbed, she regretted that she didn't break down the door. Moving from an all-female environment with the nuns to that place would have been tough enough, but then you think of all the stories that are coming out about those places now – it just broke her heart.

I remember him telling me once, 'I just dreamt about not having to go back.' To us as children, it seemed perfectly normal for them to appear and disappear, just like cousins. It didn't strike me until I got to college that some children hadn't had the childhood I had. It took me that long to realise. When he got out, he was about sixteen, and you were expected to go into an apprenticeship. You became a carpenter or a chef or something and he was going to a small little place in Tralee. My mother said to my father, 'Over my dead body – Liam, sort it!'

Helen Collins: They were going to send him to somewhere in Tralee, but my father intervened and said he was going to be properly trained and got him into Rockwell. It must have been around 1969 or 1970. Daddy had a friend involved in Rockwell, an exceptionally fine man, and this friend took Michael Peter under his wing and made sure he was properly taken care of there.

★

In St Joseph's industrial school, all the boys were expected to work, either on the farm or in the kitchens. Unsurprisingly, Michael – the only boy to voluntarily join the girls in the domestic- economy class in the Killarney orphanage – preferred the kitchens. Rockwell, however, was an institution of an entirely different stripe. A prestigious, rugby-playing boarding school for boys, it also housed a small catering college, which served the dual purposes of cooking for the fee-paying students as well as offering a decent standard of training to the catering students and ensuring they were given good work experience during the holidays. Michael himself later described it as the 'Eton College of catering', saying it gave a 'first-class training'.

Jim Bowe: The first kitchen Michael Clifford worked in was Ashford Castle and I brought him with me, I had hand-picked him, for very obvious reasons, because he had a flair. Even giving out sausages and mash, he could do it a bit different, it was amazing. So Michael came the Easter we were there.

When Michael left Rockwell, his first proper posting was cooking for an order of Jesuits in London. It was simple fare but he had his heart set on working in Claridge's. It was the only place he applied to and, after several attempts, he was offered a position working in the pastry section. It was a rude awakening to the realities of haute cuisine.

> MICHAEL CLIFFORD: I was dreaming one morning of Cork and . . . pavlova as I sculpted a potato to shape. Suddenly a muscular hand seized the nape of my neck while the other hand thrust a turned potato within an inch of my nose. 'Do you call that a potato?' intoned a furious voice. What might have passed muster in Rockwell was certainly not fit for consumption at Claridge's.

He stayed at Claridge's for three years, prospering in the pastry section before finally leaving in 1974, his reference commending him as an 'honest, sober and excellent worker'.

From there he went to the Paris Lancaster, a boutique hotel with a Michelin-starred restaurant, but his learning curve accelerated at La Peniche, Ile de France. La Peniche was a restaurant on a barge, moored opposite the Eiffel Tower, the kitchen twelve feet below the waterline, running the length of the boat. Michael worked as a commis chef in what he described as a 'hell-hole of organised chaos', serving an average of one hundred diners at lunch, one hundred and fifty at dinner, from eight in the morning until midnight. He worked on the sauce station but, if he had a spare moment, was swiftly drafted in elsewhere. 'Many a morning after making a vat apiece of eight basic sauces, I 'turned' a thousand potatoes with a knife that moved in a blur of light,' he recalled. 'France, with its passion for cooking perfection, had been a revelation. Second-best was never allowed to pass.'

This applied to produce as much as to technique, and it was a lesson Michael absorbed into his very marrow and never wavered from practising, even as national standards in his culinary university, France, began to waver and decline. Furthermore, he realised that so much of the magnificent produce he worked with could be produced just as easily in Ireland.

> MICHAEL CLIFFORD: This can be done in Ireland, I thought, and I want to do it. I want my own restaurant. I want to search out local suppliers of fresh Irish raw materials, and I want to cook with them food of the standard we cooked on the Peniche.

After Paris, he moved on to Amsterdam and his first encounter with the burgeoning nouvelle cuisine movement, its emphasis on lightness and freshness uncovering a whole new realm of knowledge. At the Ciel Bleu Restaurant, in the Japanese-owned Hotel Okura, he learned the traditional art of ice-carving from the Japanese chefs. Then he moved on to De Kersentuin. During his time there as second-in-command to the executive chef, De Kersentuin earned its

Michael Clifford

first Michelin star, and the restaurant left a deep impression on him. When he left in 1981, it was clear he had been valued.

> JOOP F. BRAAKHEKKE: Michael's professional skills contributed a great deal to the success of De Kersentuin, and I could depend on his organisational skills, especially during those hectic hours, for which he has gained the respect of his fellow workers. As Michael has become an invaluable part of our operation, we are extremely sorry to see him leave. But we realise this step is made only to further his career and therefore wish him every success in his future endeavours.

It was time for Michael to return home to Ireland.

★

> DECLAN RYAN: He was just back from Holland when I met him. He virtually had a Dutch accent at the time; he even looked Dutch, with his blonde hair. He applied for a job in the Arbutus as a chef de partie, but I could see he had the experience to do more, and grabbed him and took him up to the Cashel Palace, which I had just bought. He took over running the kitchen and did it very well.

> COLIN O'DALY: I really remember when he came to Cashel Palace. I knew Michael and Declan Ryan – it's a village industry – and they really saw his potential. He was young, single, a new kid on the block, wiry. They gave him his head and he brought new ideas, he was breaking new ground.

Despite earning a Michelin star, the Ryans sold the Cashel Palace while Michael, always hungry to learn and improve, sought further experience. He spent time in England working for the renowned Roux brothers, doing stints at the Waterside and Le Gavroche, as mentioned in Marco Pierre White's foreword in this book. He travelled armed with a reference from Declan Ryan.

> DECLAN RYAN: . . . the best young Irish chef that it has been my privilege to work with. He is an outstanding chef, extremely efficient, honest, hardworking and conscientious, and is the main reason the Cashel Palace gained a Michelin star in such a short time. His work methods, attention to detail and attention to hygiene have all been exceptional. I would whole-heartedly recommend him to any future employer.

On foot of such an encomium from a man of Ryan's professional stature, the first in the country to be awarded a Michelin star – for the Arbutus Lodge Hotel, in 1971 – it was hardly surprising Michael returned to work as head chef.

> RORY O'CONNELL: I spent the best part of a year at Arbutus under Michael

and Michel Flamme. Michael was a wonderful chef, without any shadow of a doubt, the real deal: very precise, very fair, straightforward, no ambiguity, completely committed to quality. He was very kind, there was no 'cheffy' agenda; it was just about the food. He had such a huge body of experience, it was utterly obvious, and he was very good at sharing information with his chefs, no question of that. He'd show you what was required and you'd taste it and then you knew. I learned a huge amount – it was one of the very important periods of my food learning. He was a very nice man, very sweet really. He walked at running speed everywhere, always very busy. He was a good team-builder.

To further Michael's experience, Declan Ryan paid for him to go to France on *stages* in two three-star restaurants: the world-renowned Troisgros, in Roanne, and La Bonne Auberge, in Antibes.

> DECLAN RYAN: He was very efficient, a very hard worker, very, very pleasant, even if he was very closed, and we were very saddened to hear of his untimely passing.

Michael was poached from the Arbutus, to head up a new restaurant in Dublin.

★

> COLIN O'DALY: Michael needed to spread his wings. I knew Peter and Alicia White, and White's on the Green gave him the opportunity to spread his own wings and become his own person, and he also became a darling of the media. He had his own personality and way of doing things, so it gave him an opportunity, a breakthrough point. The media started writing about him and he became his own man.

White's on the Green was where Michael Clifford became a national culinary star, albeit in more rarefied circles than now prevail in today's social-media-driven populist food revolution. White's was established by businessman Peter White and his wife Alicia, and though neither had any professional hospitality experience, their very desirable property on St Stephen's Green soon came to be described as 'the most hallowed address in gourmet Ireland'.

> PETER WHITE: We started it as a hobby. We owned the property, and I thought it would be fun. We were looking for a top chef, and we spoke to Colin O'Daly, a friend of ours, and asked him, but he had committed himself to opening his own place and pointed us in the direction of Michael – said he was a first-class chef, had the experience and background. So we went down to the Arbutus, ate there and were very impressed.
> We had a meeting in Cork, told him our plans and asked him would he be interested. He said yes and assisted us in setting up the kitchen

area and a team. He assembled a first-class crew, we left all that to him. He recruited extremely well: pastry chefs, fish chefs, he even assisted in choosing head waiters. He chose very wisely. It is not easy opening a serious restaurant from scratch, but he knew precisely the type of standards he wanted.

He was intelligent, bright but very low-key, not one of the generation of chefs who were publicity-mad. We felt his talents were not properly recognised, so we thought it a good idea to promote him, and he was very well received.

Any credit we got for the food end was entirely due to his efforts. We never had a harsh word with him. He was quiet, low-key but knew how to control a staff, and many of his team went on to open their own restaurants. He wasn't a shouter – we subsequently had chefs who were the pot-banging type – he was always in command and in control; I loved his temperament.

Many chefs are first-class at what they do but not great business people, and it is the business end that is so difficult. Perhaps if there was a weakness in Michael, that was it. We came from a business background and were very used to watching budgets and figures. But he turned up on time, did his labours long into the night, and I was very sad when I heard he'd died so young.

HELEN LUCY BURKE: Michael was very, very tough, professionally. He never cut corners, and he was continually experimenting – he was pretty cautious about having 'signature dishes'. Though people often want to know what they are going to get in a restaurant, he felt, in other hands, signature dishes fell into easy dullness. He was superb at pairing vintages and he could recall every wine, but he wasn't precious about food and drink. I loved him, he was so dedicated. What else he could have done if he had had the time, and for a long while I couldn't accept that he was gone – and the strangest thing was that he always looked so young. I was deeply attached to him; it was a terrible loss.

DAN O'MULLANE: I can still remember the lovely hazelnut and celeriac soup, a signature dish. I don't think I'd ever seen celeriac. There were no celeb chefs then, and he was quite shy in his own way but had a lovely presence. One of the up-and-coming chefs, you knew he would have his own restaurant some day.

Success on such a level allowed Michael, for the first time, some room for a life outside the kitchen. He bought a house.

LIZ COLLINS: It was in Cowper Downs, an estate where the infamous Dublin criminal Martin Cahill ('The General') also lived. All the residents woke up one morning to find the tyres on all the cars had been slashed, but he was

White's on the Green, Dublin

thrilled with his house, just thrilled to have his very first home of his own, a place he could call his own.

More importantly, he met his wife-to-be, Deirdre McGee, who, with a partner, Mary Henry, had just opened her own restaurant, JoeAllen's, in Dublin.

DEIRDRE CLIFFORD: JoeAllen's was in Leeson Street, opposite Hartigan's Pub, and I had opened it and was looking for a head chef. Chris Farrell was working with Michael in White's on the Green but he was looking for a head-chef position. Michael was away in France, on a *stage* in some restaurant and, to make a long story short, when he came back, Chris was gone. Where? To me. And Michael had never heard of JoeAllen's, even though we were getting them all in there – Charlie Haughey and all the rest of them – but to lunch; White's was the place for the evening dinner. Anyway, Michael came in looking to find out who it was that had poached his chef and he was furious at me. Eight or nine months later, we were married.

He mellowed over the years but he was tough at White's. He'd twelve or fourteen chefs, very well trained but, by God, if they didn't pull their weight there was trouble. He'd never throw pots, he was very fair, but if some of the lads had been out the night before he'd say, 'You're not switched on, I don't want you here like that, you'll burn yourself or hurt yourself', and they'd shake. Later in life he became far mellower.

ERNIE WHALLEY: I first met Michael Clifford in Stephen's Green, back in the late 1980s, just after I quit Manchester for Dublin. I remember it like it was yesterday. It was 1AM, after a function at the Shelbourne. We were introduced by Dan Mullane, of The Mustard Seed, at Adare. I had eaten Michael's cooking at White's on the Green only a couple of nights previous. A month before that, I had dined at Troisgros and understood the invisible link between what the new generation of French chefs were doing to push the envelope and what Michael was attempting at White's, where he was introducing nouvelle cuisine to a largely sceptical Irish public.

He cut an unremarkable figure, a Clark Kent sort of chef, out of the toque and apron. But he was a great innovator. I'd venture to say that, during my time in Ireland, there have only been three 'chef/influencers', these being Kevin Thornton, Johnny Cooke and Michael. The most rooted of men, when he opened Clifford's he gave us a modern Irish restaurant of a very different kind, where provenance was at the heart of the food – commonplace now, but not at the time.

PETER WHITE: I couldn't give him enough praise. He was instrumental in getting White's on the Green the recognition it received. He worked with us for about four or five years, then he decided to open his own place, as most chefs do, and we had a very amicable parting, wished him the best.

★

Michael was always going to open his own restaurant some day, and the Kerry-born chef who ended up 'from Clonakilty', according to his gravestone, very naturally gravitated to his adopted home of Cork. He and Deirdre opened Clifford's on Washington Street in Cork city on 16 September 1989. Not long after they opened, in a show of professional solidarity with one of her Euro-toques disciples, Myrtle Allen arrived with almost a dozen family members in tow, bearing a sack of orchard apples for Michael to use in the kitchen. They soon outgrew that premises and the couple purchased the old county library building on the Mardyke. With Deirdre as front-of-house manager and Michael in the kitchen, Clifford's rapidly became one of the best restaurants in the country, inundated with awards, critical accolades and popular acclaim.

DAN O'MULLANE: Deirdre was good out front and he was good in the kitchen. The symmetry created a lovely balance because he was quite shy as a man. Deirdre out front was his balancing act. Great chefs need that. We're not London, where you can have brigades and a constant customer base, and that was in the late 80s – people went out on Saturday night, and that was it in a lot of cases.

HAZEL ALLEN: I remember Myrtle bringing up all the apples when we all went [there] for a special occasion. We used to love going to the restaurant, being greeted by Deirdre, and he was a fantastic chef. It was a special place, very beautifully done, and he was such a lovely man.

DEIRDRE CLIFFORD: Local private citizens would come in with produce from their gardens and he loved that, and he'd grow his herbs out the back. They'd also bring quail, woodcock, snipe, and they'd be saying, 'Isn't it far better that someone gets the enjoyment of that dead bird?' And he shot a lot himself.

And forget your French cheeses – it was all Irish. Customers would be coming in asking for French cheeses, and Michael would nearly go for them. He hated ketchup, hated the taste, hated the idea of it, and we never had it at home. The kids would only ever eat it in other people's houses. My brother was in one time – he was a right messer – and he ordered a lamb dish. There was a little window in the door from the kitchen which Michael could look out from, and my brother pulled out a bottle of ketchup and when Michael looked out, there was my brother banging on the bottle of ketchup as if he was pouring it all over the plate. Of course, the lid was still on but Michael nearly lost his life.

ROSS LEWIS: Michael Clifford was at the front line of recognisable chefs, and I remember my father speaking very highly of him and the restaurant. My father worked in the pharmaceutical industry and entertained a lot of

24

Clifford's, Cork

clients and colleagues there. He was always keen to interlace his food with Irish produce, one of the first with a profile to do that. Most of the rest were mimicking the French style of cooking, but this was home-grown talent with genuine flair. I was thinking of becoming a chef, and my father sent me in to him for advice. I was very well-received, upstairs in a private room. He talked to me for fifteen or twenty minutes, freely giving time to this young guy. He said London was the place to go. I have very fond memories of dinner in there one night, having come back from London after becoming a chef, obviously impressed by the formality, white linen, silver – and fiercely impressed with the nice, clean, classical style of cooking. I have distinct memories of him coming around after dinner, talking to everyone. I was just about twenty-one at the time and he could have easily bypassed me, but he talked to me as well – a gentleman.

White's on the Green may have afforded Michael his first national profile, as the gifted head chef of high society's most fashionable restaurant, but Clifford's was where Michael's own culinary ethos was truly refined, a technically gifted innovator bringing his vast experience to bear on the finest Irish produce, with no seeming differentiation between 'high' and 'low'. And he became renowned as the man who elevated black pudding from mere common staple to Irish epicurean treasure.

COLETTE TWOMEY: Edward and I first met him in the late 70s, when he'd come home to visit the Collins family. And then, when he opened in Cork, he'd call in to take up supplies of our black pudding. Michael really was the pioneer, the first person to use it outside of breakfast, and he was so passionate about it and always saying what a quality, upmarket product it was, that he instilled in us a respect and a passion for it. Before, we only sold it to a few of the older customers and would have seen making it as a bit of a chore. He had a hugely positive effect on anyone he met about the black pudding.

Edward and Michael would have been very close. Deirdre was trying very hard to instil more business into him because Michael was an artiste of the highest order and maybe didn't have such a business head – his concentration was totally on his food – and Edward was trying to help him from the business point of view.

Edward passed away in October 2005, so I hadn't seen Michael for a while before he died. It was very hard to believe the two of them were gone so close together. At Michael's funeral, I brought up a black pudding as one of the offertory gifts.

★

It was while he was in Cork that Michael wrote his two cookbooks: *Cooking With Clifford: New Irish Cooking* and *Irish Bistro Cooking*. To today's reader of cookbooks, living in a golden era of production values (if not always content), they might appear inconsequential at first glance – if you can find them, that is, as they are long out of print. But there is no mistaking the author's passion for his subject matter, the polite yet firm tone of expert authority that brooks no half-measures or inferior ingredients, and the fierce belief in the primacy of local, seasonal Irish produce, infinitely ahead of its time for a culinary practitioner operating at such a rarefied level. 'I weep to think how we underuse our resources,' he wrote, recalling:

> baskets of greeny-white seakale, one of the most delicious vegetables you can eat . . . virtually unknown now on our tables though it grows wild around our coasts. Tiny wood-strawberries whose sharp intensity of flavour has never been reproduced by commercial growers . . . the spiked heads of artichokes, which are a kind of thistle and grow as freely here as their villainous cousins. Samphire grows abundantly in river estuaries and is never eaten. I cooked it when I was a chef in Holland and that wild plant commanded an enormous price. We recognise only field mushrooms, while fungi that the continentals would eat are left to rot.
>
> Our best native ingredients are seasonal – but I believe in seasonal cooking. I'm not a freezer person, though I admit it has its place. Neither am I an import person, but until oranges, lemons, bananas and passion fruit grow here, I have to conform.
>
> The great Escoffier said it all when he said, '*Faites simples*'. Or almost all, for I would amplify: make it simple and use the very best ingredients you can get of their kind.

Michael was aging his meat, hanging it in his own cold room, and putting offal on the menu every day. He pooh-poohed margarine, opting for butter and its 'incomparable flavour' every time, refusing to believe that what had been an Irish traditional ingredient since 'Stone Age times' could be bad for you.

> GEORGINA CAMPBELL: In terms of Irish cuisine, he would have been very much a key figure. Him, Gerry Galvin and John Howard, people like that, he would have been in that sphere – people who were really driven by standards, and also the first to take great pride in using Irish produce.
>
> Michael would have been very influenced by the Euro-toques ethos and would have been totally committed and passionate and determined to pass it on. White's was one of *the* restaurants – he made a real impact – but when he left for Cork he distilled that expensive fine cooking of White's down. The modest book production was a way of presenting food in this way, based very much on an understanding of people needing food as an everyday experience, and he managed to simplify his French classical training. It was a melding of classic French cooking with Irish ingredients, bringing chef skills to the concept but also making it accessible to the public. His version of Irish stew became the default recipe for Bord Bia whenever they were showcasing Irish food. He didn't see himself as being up on a cuisine pedestal.

Michael Clifford and Sally McKenna at Manning's Food
Emporium, Ballylickey

Michael Clifford demonstrating a recipe at Manning's Food
Emporium, Ballylickey

From left to right, chef Gerry Galvin, Michael and Deirdre Clifford
and hotelier Francis Brennan

BIDDY WHITE LENNON: He was an inventive and dedicated leader of a small group of young Irish chefs with classical training who shared a vision. They explored Irish food culture to combine excellent and often neglected Irish foods with their technical skills to develop what came to be known as 'new Irish cooking'. In 1990, when I was writing my first book on traditional Irish food culture, I was inspired by Michael's food. I devoted a section to 'the new tradition', demonstrating how artisan foods produced in the traditional way were being given a contemporary spin. I got to know what great company Michael the man was and shared his enthusiasm for renewing interest in Irish specialities like black pudding, spiced beef, nettle soup, smoked mackerel, rabbit and wild seakale.

★

With so many chefs, the more rarefied the atmosphere is in which they work, the greater their preference for simplicity in their downtime. This was especially true of Michael.

MICHAEL CLIFFORD: Semolina pudding and rock buns were my strong points when I was the only boy in the school taking Domestic Economy (my voluntary choice) alongside nine girls . . . But my favourite treat then was toast cut thick and spread with good beef dripping. The jellied meat juices seeped through into the soft centre and liquefied pleasantly against the tongue: to this day I am ready to put in a good word for my favourite.

LIZ COLLINS: He was a dinger for being in the chipper late at night, and I'd say, 'What are you doing eating that food?' 'Ah,' he'd say, 'I didn't have to cook, it's grand.'

TIMOTHY CLIFFORD: When he came to stay with us, his joy was to have a fry. When he first came, my wife was wondering what to cook for this 'chef', but all he wanted was beans and toast. And he loved Westerns, flopping down in front of the telly for the afternoon to watch one. He was a bit early for being a celebrity chef, but he had no pretensions about him. Outside of his profession, he had very simple tastes, a quiet pint in a small pub. Food was his passion but he kept his private life and working life very separate.

JOHN MCKENNA: The simplicity and honesty which Michael Clifford admired in food were qualities he embodied himself. He cooked for posh, wealthy people at times but it didn't faze him, and it didn't make him alter his style: his food was always honest and simple, whether there was a starched white linen tablecloth under the plate, or there wasn't.

Michael travelled with us to Paris for a dinner one year in the mid-1990s, after some of our guides had been translated into French. He cooked along with Gerry Galvin of Drimcong House, and Robbie Millar of Shanks restaurant in Northern Ireland. What I remember most about the evening was their superlative cooking, the extraordinary rudeness of our Parisian guests, and the calmness of the three chefs, transported and transplanted into a strange kitchen in a strange hotel in a strange city for an evening, and yet able to produce their very best cooking.

Michael cooked quenelles of chicken with Milleens sauce, one of his great signature dishes, and a defining dish of technique (finessed, precise) and temperament (rustic, rooted). The dish requires the cook to work hard in order to achieve something that is honest and simple.

DEIRDRE CLIFFORD: Robbie Millar, Gerry Galvin, Michael Clifford, three of them, all dead now – shocking. Gerry was good, very good, a very serious guy, but he had his hands full with Michael Clifford and Robbie Millar out in Paris and trying to get them home before the big cooking gig the next morning – and he couldn't get them home. Poor Gerry, God help him, he'd have some stories to tell. I suppose it's what happens on tour, stays on tour, but I know they were up to high jinks!

★

The Cliffords expanded, opening a bistro next door to the restaurant in an attempt to reach a wider audience but, as Deirdre admits, they were probably ahead of their time with the concept and found themselves overextended. The family relocated to Cahir, where they opened a restaurant but, again, outgrew a venue and relocated to Clonmel, trading once more as Clifford's. It was Michael's last restaurant.

GEORGINA CAMPBELL: Obviously there is the cost angle. Fine dining was limiting, going through hoops to make it more accessible to other people. The bistro offered them a restaurant business able to operate on two levels, a genuine attempt to stay in business and also to reach more people. I think these guys were pioneers, but you know what they say happens to pioneers – they get shot! It's sad. He was ahead of his time and trying so hard to bridge that gap.

★

DERRY CLARKE: I have very fond memories of Michael. When Sallyanne and I got engaged, in 1986, I took her to White's on the Green to celebrate. Michael was cooking up a storm then, and it was *the* restaurant to go to in Dublin. The food and the ambience were amazing. I was introduced to Michael that evening.

When Sallyanne and I opened in July 1989, Michael and Deirdre became regular customers at l'Ecrivain. I would sit down after they had eaten and discuss food issues, dishes, and anything restaurant-related

Robbie Millar, Michael Clifford, Gerry Galvin

Michael Clifford, in *The Consultant*, December 1992

with Michael. We would swap stories, and discuss our different cooking methods and styles. He was the first man in Ireland that I remember putting black pudding and scallops together as a dish on his menu. It is now a feature in a lot of Irish restaurants. Sallyanne and I dined in Clifford's in Cork a number of times. Again, the food was amazing, the service second to none, an unforgettable experience.

Michael gave so much to this industry and is remembered fondly by all who knew him. He was a pioneer in his day and set the bar very high for the rest of us. It is a shame he left this world when he did, but I will always remember him as the young, vibrant chef that he was.

ANDREA PETRINI: Back in '89 or '90, it may have been my first visit to Ireland, I went to his restaurant and fell in love with what he was doing. I had been brought to Ireland by literature – I was a big admirer of Irish writers – and was not expecting to find the food that I found in those days. I met Edward Twomey, who sold me some of the black pudding I had tasted in Michael's restaurants. I discovered Milleens cheese. I met Bill Hogan, the maker of the Gabriel and Desmond cheeses. I went around the country to Dublin, the North, Sligo and Galway, and it was a big astonishment to find all the good food and real personality behind the stove – most notably Michael Clifford and Gerry Galvin.

The following year, I came back and did a whole story for a French magazine, fifteen pages, on the Cork scene. There was Michael, Ballymaloe, the McKennas, the cheese. We kept in touch. When I came back the following year, Michael had opened the bistro.

In the spring of '95, the McKennas had two of their Bridgestone Guides translated into French – *100 Best Places to Eat in Ireland* and *100 Best Places to Stay in Ireland* – and me and my wife, Katarina, organised a launch in Paris with Michael Clifford, Gerry Galvin and Robbie Millar all cooking. Each one did a dish; it was a huge success. Every dish was different but, for me, Michael was the one that fitted perfectly. He was like the link between his past experiences, a very French-infused kind of cuisine in vogue for his generation, and what was starting to happen in Ireland, working with local producers in season. Michael, for me, was also ahead of what was about to happen in London in those days, where you only had Marco Pierre White turning the scene upside down.

The last time I saw him with Deirdre, we spent Christmas together at Deirdre's family home in County Louth. There was a big storm during the dinner, the lights went out and we used candles. The following morning, we discovered a huge tree had fallen just two metres away from the front door.

If Michael had been a British guy, he would have been at the forefront of modern British food. He was a master of technique and he could have applied that to British produce. He was one of the first to have a fantastic Irish cheese board, one of the first to use not only Michelin-star produce but also poorer, simpler products, like the black pudding. In Italy, black pudding has a very 'peasant' connotation and to put it into an à la carte restaurant menu was very revolutionary in those days.

★

What began as a trickle towards the end of the last century has turned into a deluge of revelations of the awful circumstances that prevailed in those institutions where the Irish State and the religious orders purported to tend to the welfare of children entrusted to their care, yet Michael barely spoke to his family about his time there and did not mention it at all to acquaintances, even friends. In fact, Michael, though charming, was notoriously reticent. To engage with others, he found a safe language in food, a code of social intercourse that allowed him to express internal passions and emotions he long ago learned to suppress. It is how he built his bond with his children, Peter and Laura – working together in the kitchen. He taught them the craft; they shared his passion.

> COLIN O'DALY: Any time you met him, the conversation was about food, things he was doing, things he was trying. It was a vocation, a way of life – that was his way. He was a quiet kind of person; he wasn't very flamboyant. He always acted in a very normal, natural way. There was never any 'on-fire' about him, and it was always food.

> DEIRDRE CLIFFORD: He even hated putting up his menus outside the restaurant. He'd see young chefs coming and he'd say, 'They're trying to pinch my ideas.' Michael would not have been great with sharing his culinary expertise with outsiders – he would if they were working with him in the restaurant – he was very protective. That would have been to do with his upbringing in the orphanage. He didn't get much, so whatever he got he held on to. He protected what he had.

> TIMOTHY CLIFFORD: I went into the air corps and when he was in Rockwell he'd visit. Or when he was in London, he would call down to Kerry. When I was in Dublin, we were always in contact then. He lived with us for a little while; he was my best man at my wedding. He was a very quiet, congenial man, social. He would be friendly to everyone. He kind of liked his independence. He'd come and go. We wouldn't even know he'd be turning up, he'd just arrive. When he worked at White's, we got to know him more then and he became very fond of our two kids – he'd come especially to see them.
>
> He would very rarely talk about his time in the institutions, and anyway, it was long before the controversy about industrial schools. It wasn't so much things weren't talked about, it just appeared there was nothing to talk about. He told me he'd been back to visit one of the brothers in Tralee and one day he mentioned one of the older boys and one of the brothers having a punch-up.
>
> That was the way we saw things, there were no long, in-depth chats

about his time there. Maybe just the odd comment like that. There was a farm there and I remember him mentioning being out working on it a few times, but mainly in the kitchen.

He was a baby and I was a toddler when he was put into the orphanage and I went to the grandparents after our mother died. We never really discussed that. We would have discussed our father's people. I would have been into genealogy.

He seemed to keep parts of his life very separate, turning up at odd times. He always kept a connection with his mother's side of the family. He'd never talk about much; he was very private but he would be there, he'd seem to turn up.

★

There was no doubting the importance to Michael of the Collins family and Clonakilty, the sole place-name inscribed on his gravestone, and he returned there time and again throughout his life, from the day he first left the industrial school in Tralee.

HELEN COLLINS: One time, he was back from Amsterdam and he was introducing my parents to this concept of mayonnaise mixed with mustard to eat with their chips. They were completely gobsmacked. He rarely cooked when he came home. Mammy was a great home cook and he adored her cooking and, anyway, he was tired of cooking, and everything she put in front of him, he'd eat.

On the rare occasion he would cook, she'd say, 'Don't put any garlic in, it repeats on Liam, on daddy.' Michael Peter would say, 'Don't worry, I'll take the little green piece in the middle out and it won't repeat on him.' My mother would say, 'I'd spend the whole day washing up after him because that's what chefs expect.' She was just as happy when he wouldn't cook.

LIZ COLLINS: In all the time I knew him, there was only one time I ever heard him raise his voice. Me and Mickey were fighting – he was fifteen and I was about twelve and Michael Peter would have been about nineteen or twenty – and he told us to pull ourselves together, we didn't know how lucky we were. That was the only time he ever got cross with us. He was a gangster, always a lovely smile across his face, and he never seemed to age.

HELEN COLLINS: We would consider him our family, and he would consider us his family. My mother loved him and my father, who did so much for us, did the same for Michael Peter. They considered Peter and Laura as two more grandchildren. Michael Peter added greatly to our lives and we were lucky to have him. This book means so much to us. It's huge to us that he's being recognised in this way.

MICHAEL CLIFFORD: As a small boy I never wanted to own a guitar and sing rhythm and blues. I never wanted to line out for Manchester United. I never wanted to be Taoiseach. I wanted to cook and I wanted this as far back as I could remember.

And cook is exactly what he did.

. . . & Son

PETER CLIFFORD: I decided to go through with the competition. I didn't even think of not going through with it. My mother and her friends said, 'Oh, you can't do it.' I never thought about it, I just said I'd continue. He was there for the first round. He helped me, showed me how to do the menu and the dishes, and I think he would have done the same. He always said, whenever you heard of a death, 'Life goes on.'

For the final, in Dublin, my cooking was almost on automatic pilot, not thinking about the loss or the death. It was like second nature, only thinking about the food. My mother, Laura, my auntie, my grandfather and the principal of my school were there, and when I won, my mother was crying. For the next three or four hours, we were hammered with newspaper reporters and journalists.

BIDDY WHITE LENNON: I was judging and we did know it was Michael Clifford's son but he was a walk-away winner when he did the final. I remember the PR company wondering would he be able for it, but he really, really focused – he put the head down.

*

There are no rules for grieving – each does it in his or her own way – but to lose a figure so central to one's life in the middle of those vulnerable teenage years is especially harrowing. Peter may have remained unnaturally calm amidst the emotional eruption that greeted his victory in the Young Chef competition but, eventually, grief found its way to the surface. How to express grief is another issue again. When you are a teenage boy, a child desperate to be a man, it is especially difficult. You certainly don't break down and weep.

DEIRDRE CLIFFORD: They were at a very vulnerable age, only fifteen. It was an awful age for both of them. I had lost the soul of my life. He had been taken away from me, and my two darlings were hurting very badly too. I was so caught up in my loss and kind of forgot that Peter and Laura were going through the same thing.

Sibling rivals cook up a storm on tight budget

By Christine Doherty

The Clifford siblings, Peter and Laura are cooking up a storm in advance of competing against each other in the Leinster final of the Tesco Young Chef of the Year.

The Ardee-based brother and sister are no strangers to either cooking or to the Tesco Young Chef of the Year.

Peter, who is 17, won the competition in 2006. He is now studying at catering college and also finds time to work in the Naremore Hotel.

His sister, who is also 17, is a pupil at Ardee Community School and is looking forward to taking home economics at Leaving Certificate level.

Peter and Laura are not twins, both of them were adopted from Romania when they were a few weeks old.

Their father, Michael Clifford, who passed away in 2006 was a Michelin chef and it seems to have been passed down.

Their mother Deirdre Clifford, is also a great cook and has always enjoyed letting her children play their part in cooking family meals.

Since the family moved to live in Ardee with their proud grandfather, Paddy

McGee he has also been able to enjoy their wonderful cooking.

For many years, the McGee family ran a well known seed and farm machinery business in Ardee.

One of Peter's specialties is rump of lamb with baby leeks, colcannon mash and fresh pea gravy.

His sister, Laura is not only a great cook, she is also becoming a talented rugby player according to her proud mother.

Both Laura and Peter qualifying for the Leinster final is a major achievement having beat off competition from hundreds of others across the province.

Leinster has proven to be a very interesting heat for the judges so far as it looks like there will be a battle on in the kitchen for the winning spots, said one of the organisers.

The Leinster Heat of the Tesco Young Chef of the Year will take place on Tuesday, April 29th in Cooks Academy, Dun Laoghaire, Co Dublin.

The eight Leinster regional finalists will be required to cook their submitted two-course menu of a starter and main course. Each will be made using an original recipe and the ingredients, which should be available in Tesco stores, must not cost more than €25.

The winners of the heat

will then go forward to compete in the national final against students from across the country.

The overall awards will be announced at a gala lunch and this year's lucky winners both winning a €3,000 family holiday voucher. Their school or college will also receive a brand new, top of the range PC.

A special prize of a weekend break in Ireland will also be awarded to the student's hardworking teacher.

This year's special prize for both winners will be a day's work experience at Derry Clarke in his Michelin-starred restaurant in Dublin to give them a taste of a chef's life.

Ardee brother and sister Peter and Laura Clifford who are competing in the Tesco Young Chef of the Year competition.

Peter and Laura Clifford competing for the 2007 Tesco Young Chef of the Year award, the year after Peter's victory

Laura Clifford winning the 2007 Tesco Young Chef of the Year award

PETER CLIFFORD: We moved to Louth after Dad died. I went to school in Dundalk to do my Junior Cert, and I began working part-time with Ray McArdle in the Nuremore Hotel. He knew my father and after he died, he took me under his wing. I was a bit of a brat back then, sixteen, didn't know where my head was after the death, I was messed up. He gave me loads of chances and kept me and trained me, gave me a platform for where I am. In my cooking career, he has been one of the most important people after my father.

Ray McArdle: He was a bit of an *enfant terrible* and his mum was having a hard time. I did take him by the scruff of the neck. He was just a young lad, an apprentice. He showed a bit of talent but people kept asking me, 'Why are you giving this kid so many chances?' Then he went on the payroll and he began to wise up. I got him into Newry College and he worked with me after college. It was to get him steady, personally, as much as to give him a job – to guide him a wee bit, to be a good influence, like a father figure.

LAURA CLIFFORD: Peter is like dad, he's not a talker, whereas I am. After dad died, me and mum sort of helped each other through it, talking and crying about it all, but Peter rebelled and wouldn't talk to anybody.

★

Eventually, after leaving catering college and Ray McArdle, the emotional dam burst and Peter left the kitchen altogether for a spell. All through his early teens, he had spent all his free time in the restaurant kitchen with his father. It was his choice but it was also his childhood surrendered and, for a while, it seemed he was finished with cooking altogether. Even when he returned to the profession, it was with a still-wounded heart, and he appeared to lack direction, moving around a lot.

It has taken several years for Peter to find his feet and regain his equilibrium but it should be borne in mind that, at the time of writing, he is still only twenty-three, with a lifetime ahead of him. But he is also a twenty-three-year-old who has more than a decade of experience in professional kitchens behind him. Apart from his technical skills and knowledge, his palate is exceptionally evolved for someone so young; that usually comes much later, if at all.

He has racked up *stages* in some prestigious restaurants in Britain, including Rick Stein's restaurant in Padstow, Jamie Oliver's Fifteen and one of Gordon Ramsey's establishments. He spent six weeks with Tom Aikens. He also spent a season with the enormously gifted Fred Cordonnier, working as his pastry chef in the very exclusive five-star Ballyfin, in County Laois.

PETER CLIFFORD: It was probably the best place I've ever worked so far and he is the best chef I've ever worked with – and that includes London as well. He's my style, probably the most passionate chef I've ever met.

41

COLIN O'DALY: I was in Bang Café one night having dinner, and dessert came out. I took a second look at it and said, 'That's no ordinary dessert,' the way it was put on the plate. I thought, that's someone who knows what he's doing. I asked the waitress who the pastry chef was and she said, 'That's Peter Clifford.' I immediately wondered if it was Michael's son, so he came on out and I met him. He's a talented chef but he needed to calm down and enjoy his cooking, because he's young – he still has a lot to learn.

During his time as the head chef in Pepper Brasserie, in Clontarf, a restaurant he helped launch, he attracted the attention of reviewers from five Irish national newspapers. (I was one of them and it was the beginning of my involvement with this book.) Of course, the only reason a twenty-three-year-old in a brand-new restaurant attracts this calibre of attention is by virtue of being the son of a culinary deity such as Michael Clifford. But that only brings them in the door; after that it's all about the food, and Peter impressed each and every one.

ERNIE WHALLEY, *SUNDAY TIMES*: It did strike me that the dish might have been inspired by Michael Clifford, as the presentation was sophisticated and the flavours mutually compatible in a way that twenty-three-year-old chefs don't often manage.

TOM DOORLEY, *Mail On Sunday*: Peter Clifford . . . is very young, has clearly inherited much of his father's talent and I suspect is wildly ambitious. Peter's cooking, filtered through the prism of practicality in a neighbourhood joint . . . is good without being knockout, beat-a-path-to-the-door stuff. But give him time and a different location and I suspect there will be culinary fireworks.

ROSS GOLDEN-BANNON, *THE SUNDAY BUSINESS POST*: There's some really stunning food on offer here, even the more workaday dishes are created with care . . . Peter Clifford's cooking deserves some white tablecloths and a very long queue of customers.

LUCINDA O'SULLIVAN, *SUNDAY INDEPENDENT*: Brasserie and grill may be the theme here but it hasn't stopped Clifford from displaying his skills by adding some top-notch twists.

JOE MCNAMEE, *IRISH EXAMINER*: Peter Clifford is much more than a chip off the old block and very definitely one to watch.

★

Peter and Laura arrived into Michael and Deirdre's life in 1991.

DEIRDRE CLIFFORD: Michael always wanted to adopt. We used to watch recordings of various programmes after the restaurant had closed and late one night we sat down and watched *Today Tonight* with Brian Farrell and it was about the orphanages in Romania. We both decided we'dbetter do something – even talked about the possibility of adopting. Because a lot of pharmaceutical companies used the restaurant, I managed to organise to bring medical aid out to Romania and I went out there for eight weeks on my own.

I came across little Peter in one orphanage where he'd been abandoned and found Laura in another orphanage. There was a whole process to go through, being cleared by the guards and so on, and we had great help from Mary Banotti and Nora Owen, who were related to the Collinses.

They're not blood siblings, but there is only nine days between them so we thought of them as being twins. Not long after we got back, I was in Paul Street Shopping Centre, in Cork, with them in a double-buggy, and we met an old woman who was gushing over them and putting the coin on their head for luck and so on. When she heard there was only nine days between them, she said, 'Oh, Jesus, love! That was a terrible labour!'

*

PETER CLIFFORD: Growing up with dad, our shared time was in the kitchen. But when he was off, every week, we'd always go for a family meal to a restaurant and, on the other day, mother would cook at home. Outside of the kitchen, it was family time for the four of us.

LAURA CLIFFORD: Every time I went into the kitchen, dad would be telling me to get out, you're distracting the staff. And I would be. I'd be tasting stuff, talking to them all, distracting them. Peter would be quiet, watching and working, and I'd be getting in the way.

My time with dad used to be more when he was off from the kitchen. We'd go to Tom Skinny's in town for our pizza, go for a walk or swimming together. If we were away in a hotel as a family, me and dad would be up early for breakfast while mum and Peter slept on upstairs. He was my role model, my actual hero.

PETER CLIFFORD: He bought me my first gun when I was fifteen. I always liked that, going out shooting with him, coming back and cooking whatever we caught. We always had dogs, one an excellent gun dog, Jilly, for shooting, a dropper. For practice, he had her carry a semi-inflated balloon, so when she was carrying a pheasant she'd do it lightly, not bruised. I sold my two guns after he died but it's something I'll go back to eventually.

★

Peter's 'apprenticeship' was exceptional beyond compare, beginning before he even hit his teens, working in a professional kitchen under the watchful eye of one of Ireland's greatest-ever chefs, his own father.

> PETER CLIFFORD: He never sat me down to tell me anything. I was just watching everything. He showed me all the basics from the age of ten, eleven, twelve: chopping, stocks, sauces. I wasn't treated like a son or a favourite, I was just another member of staff, washing dishes or whatever, saucing on the pass at the start and then, when it started getting serious, he put me over with the pastry chef and that's where I got my love of desserts.

> LAURA CLIFFORD: When we were younger, the roles used to be reversed. Mum used to laugh about it. I was mad into sport and played rugby and, on a Saturday morning, I'd be getting into my rugby gear and Peter would be getting dressed to go and work in the kitchen. When we were younger, we always said we'd have a Michelin-star restaurant together when we grew up, me doing front of house and Peter in the kitchen.

> DEIRDRE CLIFFORD: He'd come back from school, there'd be no homework done, the bag would be thrown down and he'd be into the kitchen. I'd be saying to Michael, 'He's got to do his homework,' and Michael would say, 'He's OK, he's in the kitchen with me.' I was all about him getting the education – and I suppose he did, the same way Michael did, really. We all worry about books and school but, in fact, it worked out for the best in the end.

★

People always spoke of Michael's reticence. They never failed to mention his gentle charm, but they always mentioned his quiet, almost secretive manner as well, and that he was only truly animated when speaking about food. Peter, too, can be like that – watchful, listening – but when the conversation turns to food, he can't be stopped.

> PETER CLIFFORD: I'm like him, like that. If you were talking to my sister, Laura, she'd talk away, but I am quite like him. Like him, I hate Christmas, birthdays, presents, even showing affection. Like me, he didn't like to express his feelings. Him being affectionate was sharing his knowledge with me in the kitchen, having me beside him in the kitchen. When I won the competition, I knew he was happy but he just said, 'Well done, Peter, concentrate on the final.'

★

Peter and his partner, Helen, have a little boy: Michael Peter.

> PETER CLIFFORD: Having a child that young, you have to learn quickly.
> It was hard, but I wouldn't regret it. Michael was always going to be
> Michael Peter. A lot of people call me Michael Peter: all the Collinses
> call me Michael Peter, Colin O'Daly calls me Michael Peter.

★

Finally, I feel it is essential to make absolutely clear this is not the book Peter Clifford initially imagined. He never set out with a desire to see his name or picture on the cover. Certainly, he is driven and ambitious but is also aware his industry recognises achievement only, not artifice. Michael's reputation and renown was founded on years of backbreaking toil, a voracious desire to learn and a single-minded focus on food, even before he was presented with the opportunity to shine in his own right.

The goal Peter, Laura and Deirdre first formulated after Michael's death was to have Michael's two cookbooks republished. But the format of this book takes the initial idea a step further and, personally, I feel it is the correct decision – making the difference between a memorial and a living legacy. It exhumes not just Michael's reputation and renown but also his recipes, revealing them to be equally of their time yet timeless.

They allow us to see the connection between father and son and, despite Peter's current youthful obsession with some of the more glamorous tricks of the trade, I have a feeling this continued engagement with his father's culinary legacy will bring further discipline to his cooking. And someday, if Peter is lucky enough to achieve his dream of having his own restaurant, young Michael Peter might work alongside him. The restaurant, of course, will have to be called Clifford & Son.

> PETER CLIFFORD: I want to cook really good food and build respect for my
> abilities as a chef, learn as much as possible and learn the business side
> of it, learn how to be a restaurateur as well and gain more experience.
> Keep learning, keep cooking, keep getting better. I have a very long way
> to go before I'm anywhere as good as my dad but I'll keep trying every
> day and I reckon this book will help others to understand what my mum,
> Laura and me know well – that the great chef Michael Clifford was also
> a great husband and father and we still miss him. This is one way of
> keeping his memory alive.

RECIPES

1

BREADS

BLACK OLIVE BREAD

3 LARGE LOAVES OR 12 TO 15 SMALL LOAVES

This is my own recipe, which I came up with about three years ago. It came from a recipe we used in Ballyfin, where I was chef Fred Cordonnier's pastry chef. I was there for a season and it was amazing. Fred's a bit of a genius. This recipe is just a plain French dough with olives added. Weigh the dough and divide it into equal portions. Close to 50g is a good guide, or make two or three larger loaves by dividing the overall weight by two or three.

—Peter Clifford

INGREDIENTS

10g fresh yeast

12g honey

175ml tepid water

A drizzle of olive oil

315g strong flour

6g salt

50g pitted black olives, chopped

METHOD

In a mixing bowl, dissolve the yeast and honey in the water and oil. Separately mix the flour, salt and olives. Pour the liquid mixture into the dry. Combine together until a dough is formed. Knead the dough until it becomes smooth and elastic (about 5 minutes using a processor with a dough hook or about 10 minutes by hand). Let it prove at room temperature until the dough has doubled in size. Don't speed up the proving by leaving the dough in a warm place, as the flavour will develop by proving it slowly. Be patient; this could take up to two hours. Knock the dough down by kneading until the air is removed.

Shape the dough and let it prove one more time on a baking tray. Score the loaves widthways, leaving 5cm between each cut. Use a very sharp knife (pros use a lame with disposable razor blades) and bake at 215° Celsius for at least 12 minutes for small loaves or 20 minutes for large loaves, or until a crust is formed and there's a hollow sound when you tap the base of the loaf.

CARROT BREAD

2 LARGE LOAVES

This carrot bread is very nice to use instead of brioche with a piece of foie gras, toasted or not. It's also a great replacement for brioche in a mixed-bread basket. The carrots give it a sweetness and the yoghurt gives it a freshness. We did a parsnip bread in Ballyfin. There was a lot of trial-and-error stuff there, messing around.

—Peter Clifford

INGREDIENTS

20g fresh yeast

150ml milk at room temperature

2 medium eggs, slightly beaten

50g vegetable oil

300g carrots, peeled, cooked and mashed

30g fresh yogurt

500g strong flour

15g caster sugar

15g salt

50g oats

METHOD

Prepare two loaf tins by greasing them with butter. Preheat the oven to 170° Celsius. Dissolve the yeast in the milk. Add the eggs, oil, yoghurt and carrots. Separately, mix the flour, sugar, salt and oats. Add the dried mixture to the liquid and knead for about 10 minutes. The dough should be wet and sticky. Divide it between the two tins and bake for at least 30 minutes, or until the base makes a hollow sound when tapped.

BLUE CHEESE AND POTATO BREAD

2 LOAVES

Dad used to use Cashel Blue an awful lot, but I prefer Crozier Blue, which is a little bit sweeter. I developed this recipe in Pepper, in the early days, when we first opened. It's a nice soup bread, fresh and not too strong if you're not a big fan of blue cheese.

—Peter Clifford

INGREDIENTS

30g fresh yeast
100ml tepid water
200g mashed potatoes
2 eggs, beaten
100ml vegetable oil
200g blue cheese
600g strong flour
70g sugar
15g salt

METHOD

In a bowl, dissolve the yeast in the water. Add in the mashed potatoes, eggs, oil and cheese and stir until everything is incorporated. Add the flour, sugar and salt. Knead until smooth: 10 minutes by hand or 5 using a processor with a dough hook. Let the mixture prove at room temperature until it has doubled in size. Knock the air down from the dough by kneading it slightly. Shape it into two loaves and let it prove for another 20 to 30 minutes. Bake at 170° Celsius for at least 30 minutes, or until the base makes a hollow sound when tapped.

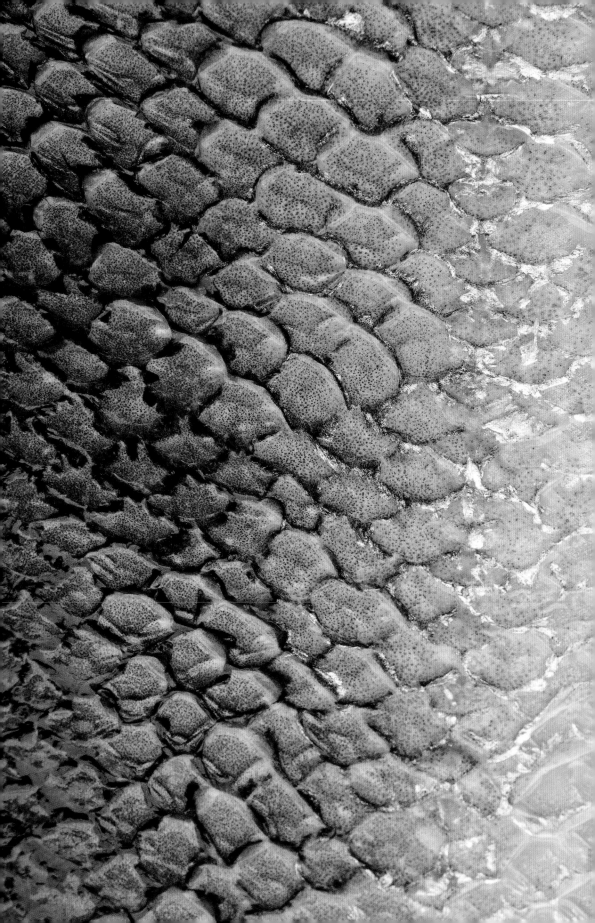

2

STARTERS

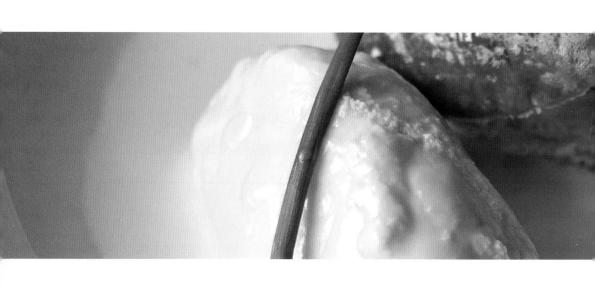

CHICKEN QUENELLES WITH MILLEENS CHEESE
SERVES 6

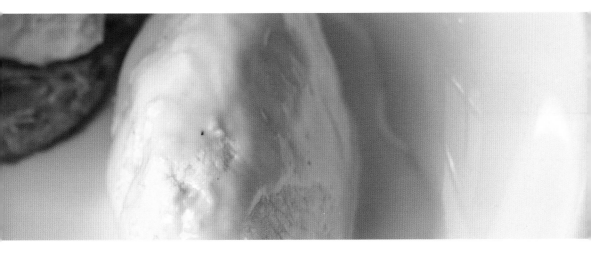

People will always associate my dad with Clonakilty Blackpudding but this was really his signature dish. He got the idea from Vettard, in Lyon, where they are famous for their quenelles. They use pike but he decided to try chicken. He came up with it one day in the kitchen in Clifford's, on the Mardyke. My mum remembers him cutting out the plastic to make the mould for the hen pastry shape that went on top.

I've eaten it since I was a kid but the first time I tried making it, I actually did it as a terrine. There was enough to feed the Irish army but it didn't work, it wasn't very good. In the Market Bar, the first place where I was in charge of the kitchen, I made it and put it on the menu. I made it exactly to his recipe, no tweaks, and it was perfect. I've never touched the quenelle recipe, although I play with the garnish quite a lot.

This dish feels like the biggest connection I have with him, food-wise, and I've adopted it as my own signature dish. It is one of his strongest dishes: very clever, well-balanced, light. To those of us who knew him, it was probably his best. It was never off his menu after he came up with it.

—Peter Clifford

Be warned! Put on a music tape, take the phone off the hook and disconnect the doorbell, for quenelles demand a strong arm, a fine but resistant sieve and endless patience.

—Michael Clifford

Ingredients

Puff Pastry Discs
300g puff pastry

Quenelles
250g chicken breast
1 egg white
300ml fresh cream
Lemon juice
25g Milleens cheese, chilled,
  rind removed, diced
Chicken stock,
  for poaching

Sauce
1 small shallot, diced
1 knob of butter
100ml white wine
250ml chicken stock
150ml fresh cream
15g Milleens cheese, rind
  removed, diced

Method

Cut the puff pastry into six discs, each approximately 7cm in diameter. Bake them for 10 to 12 minutes at 180° Celsius until golden brown. Slice them through the middle, yielding 'top' and 'bottom' discs to sandwich the quenelle.

Place chicken breast in liquidiser. Add the egg white and 100ml cream. Remove and pass through a sieve. Place into a stainless steel bowl over ice. Add remaining cream and lemon juice. Place in the fridge to rest for half an hour to relax and make it easier to work with.

Pre-heat the oven to 170° Celsius and put the chicken stock on to heat up. Use a 'white' chicken stock made from raw chicken carcass, which gives a clear stock. If you poach the quenelles in a 'brown' chicken stock, they will lose their lovely whiteness.

Using two dessert spoons, form egg-shaped quenelles. With a small spoon, place a small piece of Milleens cheese in the centre of the quenelle. Continue in this way until the mixture is used up. Place in a shallow ovenproof dish and cover with hot chicken stock. Simmer in the oven until the quenelles are firm, about 12 to 15 minutes.

To make the sauce, sweat the shallot with a knob of butter. Add the white wine and chicken stock and reduce by half. Add cream and reduce until it coats the back of a spoon. Whisk the Milleens cheese in and pass the mixture through a fine sieve. Adjust seasoning to taste.

To serve, place the bottom half of a pastry disc on a plate, three quenelles per serving on top, and pour the sauce over and around and 'close the sandwich' with the top half of the pastry disc. Garnish with chopped chives.

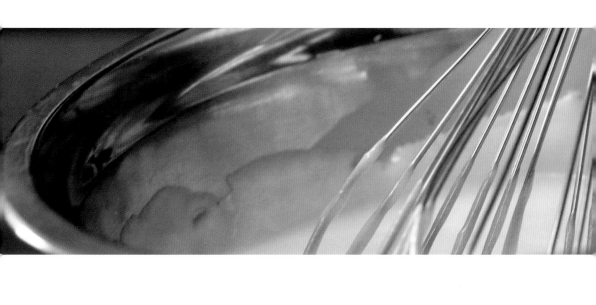

TRIPE-AND-ONION SOUFFLÉ

SERVES 4

My mum remembers that the older generation of diners at Clifford's, in Cork, would have eaten this. My dad had the punters for it, people who would have tried it before ever coming in to him. Almost everyone in Cork would have eaten tripe at some stage. Dad was very passionate about eating local produce, long before most others, but this wasn't a conscious attempt at 'nose-to-tail eating'. Eating tripe would have been second nature growing up in Cork.

—Peter Clifford

INGREDIENTS

200g tripe

½ a medium onion

450ml milk

30g *beurre manié*

1 egg yolk

4 egg whites

2 tbsp grated cheddar cheese
(Hegarty's, made in Cork, is
excellent)

1 tbsp chopped parsley

METHOD

Wash the tripe and cut it into small cubes. Place the tripe in a saucepan with the onion and the milk. Simmer for 45 minutes. Strain the milk into another saucepan, bring to the boil and whisk in *beurre manié*. Cool slightly and stir in the egg yolk. Whisk the egg whites with a pinch of salt until stiff and fold gently into sauce mixture.

Butter a large soufflé dish and half-fill with the soufflé mixture. Then, in the centre, add tripe and onion and cover with the remaining mixture. Sprinkle with cheese and parsley.

Cook at 165° Celsius for 13 minutes or until ready: nicely risen, slightly browned. Serve immediately. It's delicious just on its own, but a light green salad and a little crusty baguette would be wonderful additions.

Note: *Beurre manié* is equal parts flour and butter mixed together into a dough. Store it in the fridge wrapped in cling film for up to a week. You can also drop little knobs of it into soups, stews and casseroles near the end of the cooking process to thicken them up.

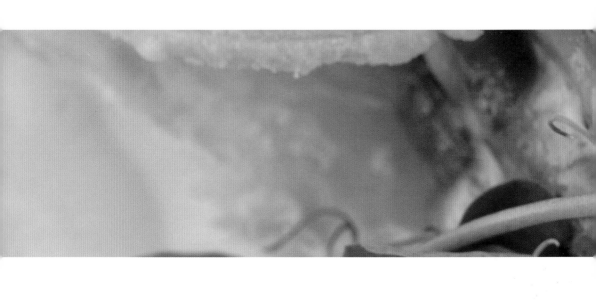

FEUILLETTE OF ASPARAGUS WITH LEMON-BUTTER SAUCE
SERVES 4

Dad used to do this dish with rectangular cushions of pastry, but I like using something closer to a circle. Do whatever works best for you. Lay the sheet of pastry out flat and cut it into four pieces of equal size – each about the size of an adult's palm – and bake. I've done this as a vegetarian option in several restaurants, and I did it as part of an eight-course tasting menu for a private dinner party in Rahanna House, in Ardee, back in 2008. This dish is best around May when you can use fresh, local asparagus. The imported asparagus you get during the rest of the year just cannot compare to the Irish stuff.

—Peter Clifford

Ingredients

Sauce
30ml white wine vinegar
30ml white wine
2 shallots, finely chopped
225g unsalted butter
10ml lemon juice
4 white peppercorns,
 crushed

Pastry and Asparagus
250g puff pastry
16 stems fresh asparagus

Garnish
Pea shoots or fresh herbs

Method

Place the vinegar, white wine and shallots in a saucepan over a moderate heat. Bring to the boil and reduce by about half. Gradually add the butter, in small pieces, whisking each piece in thoroughly. The mixture should be creamy in consistency. Season with crushed pepper and salt, add lemon juice and pass through a sieve.

Poach the asparagus in boiling salted water until tender. Do not overcook. Using a serrated knife, slice each of the four pre-baked puff-pastry cushions in half to create a sandwich effect.

Arrange the asparagus on one of the cushions and spoon the sauce over the asparagus and on the plate around the cushion. Cover with the top half of the puff pastry 'sandwich'. Garnish with pea shoots or fresh herbs.

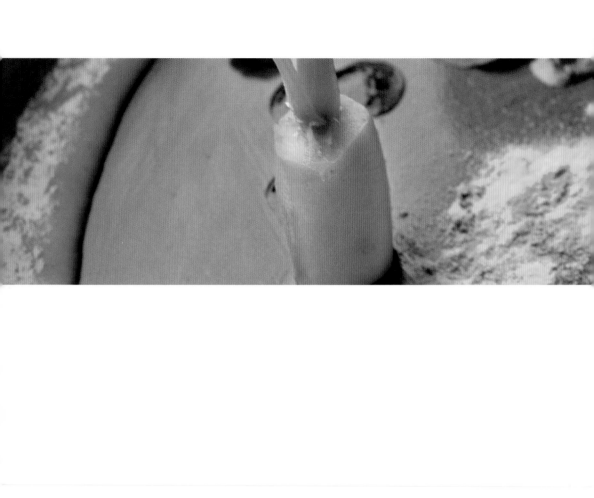

MODERN CRUBEEN 'CROQUETTE' WITH CARROT PURÉE

SERVES 4

This is my version of something Fred Cordonnier was doing in Ballyfin. My version is moister.

—Peter Clifford

INGREDIENTS

Crubeen
8 pigs' trotters
2 carrots
1 celery stalk
1 onion
1 tomato
2 cloves garlic
4 cloves
1 bay leaf
½ tbsp ground black pepper

Carrot Purée
25g unsalted butter
300g small carrots,
  peeled and chopped
2 star anise
200ml chicken stock
100ml cream
Juice of 2 lemons
4g caster sugar
2 sprigs tarragon

Croquette Filling
2 tbsp very finely diced carrot,
  celery and parsley
2 tbsp Dijon mustard
75ml dry white wine

Croquette Coating
200g flour
4 eggs, well beaten
200g fine breadcrumbs
  (panko crumbs are excellent
  if you can get them)

METHOD

To cook the pigs' trotters, place them with the carrots, celery, onion, tomato, garlic, cloves, bay leaf and black pepper in a large pot of water and bring to a gentle boil, then turn down to a simmer. Skim off any scum that rises to the top and cook on a low heat for 3 to 4 hours, until the meat falls off the bone. When cool enough to handle, pick off all the meat, skin and everything else, discarding only the bones.

To make the carrot purée, melt the butter in a saucepan over a low heat, then sweat the carrots for 4 to 5 minutes with the star anise. Add the chicken stock, cream, lemon juice, sugar and tarragon, and cook until the carrots are soft, 6 to 8 minutes. Remove the star anise, put the mixture in a blender and blend to a smooth purée. Warm through very gently when ready to serve.

To finish the croquettes, mix the picked meat with the finely diced vegetables and parsley, mustard, wine and seasoning. Lay this mixture out onto a sheet of cling film, bringing it roughly into a sausage shape with your hands. Bring the cling film up and over the mix and roll it into a sausage shape, twisting both ends until it forms a very tight, firm tube of filling. Place in the fridge to set for two hours.

Once the filling is set, cut it into 4cm lengths. You could reshape them into balls, but if you are handling them excessively they will need to rest again in the fridge for a further 20 to 30 minutes. Roll these in flour, then eggs, then breadcrumbs, and set aside in the fridge until ready to cook. To cook, deep-fry at 170° Celsius for 4 to 5 minutes until golden brown and rising to the top of the cooking oil.

Serve with warmed carrot puree and maybe some salad but you can also add other garnishes. In the version cooked for the accompanying picture, I added some whole steamed carrot, onion relish, marinated raisins and fresh watercress.

MUSHROOM BROTH WITH A MUSHROOM DUMPLING

SERVES 4 TO 6

This was developed by myself and my sous-chef at the time. This is a very classy starter, and it's a dish I could very easily picture my dad serving in somewhere like White's on the Green. The dumplings are made by adding a duxelles and a mushroom purée to the dumpling mix. It might seem a bit long-winded but, I promise you, it's really worth the effort.

—Peter Clifford

Dumplings
250ml water
115g butter, softened
125g plain flour
4 whole eggs
10g Parmesan, grated
2tbsp tarragon, chopped

Duxelles
150g wild mushrooms, very
  finely diced
15g butter

Mushroom Purée
150g wild mushrooms
15g butter
20ml water

Dark Mushroom Stock
500g wild mushrooms
1.2l water
75g shallots, diced
1 tbsp chopped tarragon
1 sprig thyme

White Mushroom Stock
500g white button mushrooms
1.5l water
1 onion, diced
2 celery sticks
1 large carrot, peeled and
  chopped
1 tbsp chopped tarragon
1 clove garlic
1 sprig thyme

METHOD

To start the dumplings, place the water and butter in a pot and bring to a boil. Add the flour and, stirring continuously with a wooden spoon, cook this mixture until it comes away from the sides of the pot. Remove from the heat. When cool, beat the eggs in, one at a time, mixing well between each one. Set aside.

Make the duxelles by sautéing the mushrooms in a hot pan with the butter for 4 to 5 minutes and then seasoning with salt. Start the mushroom purée by sautéing the mushrooms in a hot pan with the butter until the mushrooms are tender, about 4 to 5 minutes. Season with salt, place in a blender, add the water and blend until you have a very smooth purée. Pass the purée through a fine sieve.

Now combine the duxelles and the mushroom purée with the grated cheese and tarragon and beat into the dumpling mixture until fully incorporated. Season with salt. Quenelle the mushroom-dumpling mix by using two spoons to shape the mixture into nice ovals. Place these quenelles into a pot of simmering, salted water. When they float to the top, they are ready. Remove them and keep them warm.

To make the dark mushroom stock, place the mushrooms, water, shallots, tarragon and thyme in a large pot, bring to the boil and simmer for 30 minutes. Pour through a fine sieve and set aside in a jug. When the cloudy residue has settled to the bottom (10 or 15 minutes), decant very gently into another container, taking extra care to leave the cloudy residue behind.

To make the white mushroom stock, combine the mushrooms, water, onion, celery, carrot, tarragon, garlic and thyme in a large pot and bring to a boil. Let this mixture simmer for 50 minutes. Pass through a sieve into another pot, add the dark mushroom stock and then bring this to a simmering boil, allowing it to reduce and concentrate for a further 15 minutes.

To serve, ladle the broth into a large bowl and gently drop a dumpling into the broth. This can be garnished with a few sautéed wild mushrooms and some fresh tarragon leaves.

MICHAEL'S NETTLE SOUP
Serves 4 to 6

This would have always been on my dad's menu in May, when the nettles are younger and sweeter, not too stringy. It was one of the dishes my sister Laura did when she entered the Young Chef of the Year competition. The judges said they liked that she was using indigenous, wild food. It's a nice light soup, very fresh, well-balanced and inexpensive – and very Irish. I like using nettles. I even have a lamb dish using nettles in the accompanying sauce. The trick to this soup is to use a nice floury potato. Don't worry if you don't have a full *bouquet garni*. Just a few sprigs of fresh thyme and a fresh bay leaf will do very nicely.

—Peter Clifford

This soup is ideally served with brown bread.

—Michael Clifford

Ingredients

1 large onion
1 leek, washed and chopped
1 clove of garlic
1 knob of butter
75g nettle leaves, blanched
  and chopped
2 medium potatoes, peeled
  and washed
1.25l chicken stock
1 *bouquet garni* (thyme, bay
  leaf, rosemary, parsley, sage)
250ml cream

Michael's Garnish
50ml lightly whipped cream
½ tsp of Irish whiskey

Peter's Garnish
Wild garlic-infused cream

Method

Sweat the onion, leek and garlic in a knob of butter and add nettles, potatoes and chicken stock with the *bouquet garni*. Simmer for 15 to 20 minutes. Remove the *bouquet garni* and then liquidise and pass through a fine sieve. Add cream and return to the boil. Simmer for another 2 to 3 minutes and adjust seasoning to taste. Garnish with a spoon of whiskey or wild garlic-flavoured cream on each serving.

ARTICHOKE SOUP AND FOIE GRAS MOUSSE, WITH PEAR AND HAZELNUTS

SERVES 4

This is a great winter soup when Jerusalem artichokes are in season, very Christmassy. I had it on the menu in Pepper Brasserie last Christmas and it was very popular. Looking at the list of ingredients, I think my dad would have been much more comfortable with this one than with some of my other dishes! The garnishes should be done well in advance of serving and will hold; they will keep in the fridge for twenty-four hours.

—Peter Clifford

INGREDIENTS

Artichoke Soup
8 Jerusalem artichokes, scrubbed
  and peeled
2 cloves of garlic, roughly
  chopped
1 shallot
25g to 30g butter
500g chicken stock
70ml cream
30ml lemon juice

Foie Gras Mousse
250g foie gras, diced
150ml single cream
2 eggs
10ml Madeira

Hazelnuts
100g hazelnuts

Pear Garnish
Juice of 1 lemon
1 pear, very ripe

METHOD

Wash, peel and slice the artichokes. If you peel them with a teaspoon, you'll lose a lot less of the valuable flesh under the skin. Chop the garlic and the shallot. Sauté the artichokes, garlic and shallot in the butter for 4 to 5 minutes, without colouring. Add the stock. Cook the artichokes until tender. Blend the soup, pass through a fine sieve, season with salt and add lemon juice and cream.

For the mousse, mix the foie gras, cream and eggs together in a food blender. Add seasoning to taste and a little Madeira. Pour into a container: it must be 2cm to 3cm deep. Cover with cling film and put in the oven at 85° Celsius for 15 to 20 minutes. It should be wobbly, like a crème brûlée, when it comes out of the oven. Once it's cool, put it in a piping bag, ready to pipe into bowls, or form into quenelles, or you can simply spoon it in.

Roast the hazelnuts in the oven at 160° Celsius. Check after 4 or 5 minutes. The skin should easily flake off the nut but be careful if tasting one, as they will be very hot. Remove from the oven, place in a dry tea towel and rub together to remove as much skin as possible. Halve or chop roughly and set aside to use as a garnish. Quarter the pear lengthways, remove the pips and dice or slice. Place in a bowl and cover with water and lemon juice to prevent browning. Set aside to use as a garnish.

To serve, place some pear in the centre of a wide, shallow soup bowl. Pipe or spoon some foie gras mousse on top, gently ladle soup around and sprinkle hazelnuts on top.

APPLE-AND-CHESTNUT SOUP
SERVES 6

My dad used to put this soup on the Christmas menus, using orchard apples. Mum remembers that, not long after they opened in Washington Street, Myrtle Allen turned up with about twelve family members, to give them a bit of a boost as they were just starting out, and she brought along a big sack of Irish orchard apples for my dad to use in the kitchen. I've made this soup as an amuse-bouche in Pepper and I had it on the Christmas menu as well. Fresh chestnuts can be difficult to source in Ireland so we use pre-prepared, but we used to always get apples – especially when we lived in Cahir and Clonmel – from Con Traas at The Apple Farm.

—Peter Clifford

Ingredients

Knob of butter

100g shallots, diced

2 large Irish orchard apples

½ dozen chestnuts,
  pre-peeled and roasted

180g peeled potatoes, diced

1l chicken stock

100ml cream

Method

Melt the butter and then add the shallots, apples and chestnuts. Cook until the shallots have softened and the apple is breaking down and then add the diced potatoes. Season, and then add the chicken stock and simmer for about 30 minutes. Liquidise all the ingredients and then pass through a fine sieve. Season again, if necessary, and then add cream.

BEEF CONSOMMÉ FLAVOURED WITH TOMATO AND CHERVIL

SERVES 6

This is a recipe my dad came up with in White's, but the first time I ever did it was in Pepper. It's light, the chervil works really well with the beef, and the tomato really freshens it up. I like chervil. You don't see it that often but it is a very versatile herb, maybe a bit old fashioned to some people, but a great taste never goes out of style. I don't always use the Madeira or port, but it certainly adds a little old-school pep.

—Peter Clifford

4 to 5 tomatoes, peeled,
  seeded and very finely diced

225g lean minced beef

2 egg whites

1 large bunch of chervil,
  leaves picked from stalks

1.5l brown beef stock

Bouquet garni or sprigs of
  fresh thyme and rosemary

170g finely chopped mixed
  vegetables (onion, leek,
  carrot, celery)

To peel and deseed the tomatoes, make four shallow cuts in each, just through the outer skin, from top to bottom. Drop them into a pot of boiling water for about 10 to 15 seconds, take them out of the water and peel off the skin. Slice the tomatoes into quarters and scrape out seeds with a spoon. Reserve four quarters to be used for garnish. Dice the remainder into very small pieces, almost pulp.

Thoroughly mix the beef, egg whites, tomato pulp, chervil stalks and seasoning. Add this to the cold stock along with the chopped vegetables, and stir well. Add the *bouquet garni* or herbs. Place over a gentle heat and gradually bring to the boil, stirring occasionally. When the mixture boils, turn down the heat and simmer very gently. (Never stir a consommé after it comes to the boil or it will cloud.) Simmer for approximately 45 minutes.

When ready, leave aside to settle for about 10 minutes. Strain carefully through a sieve (lined with muslin if you have it). Dice the reserved tomato flesh and roughly chop the chervil, for garnish. The flavour can be enhanced with the addition of a few drops of Madeira or port before serving.

GATEAU OF CLONAKILTY BLACKPUDDING
SERVES 4

This is the dish that people probably associate with my dad the most. He elevated black pudding from being seen as a breakfast dish to being seen as a proper fine-dining restaurant dish. He'd first have met Eddie and Colette Twomey, who owned the Clonakilty Blackpudding company, when he was a young boy in Clon, and they remained lifelong friends.

Mum remembers that when it first came on the menu, in the Washington Street Clifford's, the reaction was simply unbelievable, not only from the local people in Cork, but also from the critics. National and international critics, the likes of Andrew Lloyd Webber, all absolutely loved it. It even won a competition in an English women's magazine. They published a load of recipes and asked readers to try them all and nominate their favourite, and his was the winning recipe.

—Peter Clifford

My gateau of Clonakilty Blackpudding uses simple ingredients which are easily available, but oh!—the difference they make to this lovely honest food. Try it.

—Michael Clifford

Ingredients

3 large potatoes (waxy ones
   are best for this recipe)

1 cooking apple

200g mushrooms

1 clove of garlic

16 slices of Clonakilty
   Blackpudding

25g smoked bacon, diced

10ml sherry vinegar

50ml chicken stock

Butter

Method

Peel and parboil the potatoes. They should be firm enough to slice thinly without falling apart. Set them aside. Cook the apple in a knob of butter, without colouring it. Sauté the mushrooms with sliced garlic. Place the apple and mushrooms in a liquidiser. Purée and set aside.

Slice the potatoes very thinly and arrange in a fan shape (about 8 slices per portion) on a baking tray lined with greaseproof paper. Brush with melted butter and season well with salt and milled pepper. Glaze under the grill until golden brown.

Fry the pudding and bacon in a pan until the bacon is crispy. Reheat the apple-and-mushroom mixture. Add a knob of butter and season well.

To make the sauce, deglaze the bacon-and-black pudding pan with sherry vinegar and reduce by half. Add the chicken stock, bring to a low boil, and whisk in a knob of butter.

To assemble the dish, using a spatula, place a potato fan on each plate. Add a layer of purée, then pudding and top with another potato fan. Place a small quenelle of mushroom purée on top. Place bacon around the outside of the plate. Pour sauce around the finished dish.

CLONAKILTY BLACKPUDDING WITH PURÉE OF MUSHROOMS, SERVED WITH BLINIS

SERVES 4

My dad will be forever associated with Clonakilty Blackpudding. He had a very close personal relationship with Eddie and Colette Twomey, the makers of this renowned black pudding, and at his funeral, Colette brought up a piece as one of the offertory gifts. This was a starter that was conceived in the bistro in the Mardyke. I did it in the Market Bar for the first time. It's a nice brunch-y dish. The recipe below uses the standard-size black pudding most commonly available in the shops, but feel free to use a little less or a little more.

—Peter Clifford

INGREDIENTS

Mushroom Purée
1 clove of garlic
1 shallot
400g button mushrooms

Blinis
30g buckwheat flour
30g plain flour
Pinch of salt and sugar
30g fresh yeast
10ml warm water
5ml vegetable oil
1 egg yolk
50ml milk, warmed
1 egg white

Black Pudding
280g black pudding

Sauce
20ml sherry vinegar
250ml chicken stock
1 knob of butter

METHOD

For the mushroom purée, dice the garlic, shallot and mushroom and sauté in a little butter. Season well to taste. Purée in a processor and set aside.

For the blinis, combine both flours with salt and sugar. Dissolve the yeast in the water. Add the yeast to the flour mixture. Add the oil and egg yolk, and season. Gradually add the warm milk. Cover and leave in a warm area for approximately 30 minutes, until the batter is thick. Whip the egg whites and fold into the mixture. Fry the blinis in a little butter until golden brown on both sides.

Separately, fry the black pudding slices in hot pan with a little butter. To assemble the dish, place mushroom purée in the centre of the plate. Put black pudding slices on top. For the sauce, add the sherry vinegar and chicken stock to the black-pudding pan with a knob of butter and reduce by half. Pour over the finished dish and serve with blinis.

WINTER SALAD WITH SPICED BEEF, AVOCADO AND BLUE CHEESE, SCENTED WITH WALNUT OIL

SERVES 4

My mum remembers my dad getting the spiced beef from the English market, from Flynn's. Even when he did a spiced-beef dish with mango and ginger sauce in White's on the Green, he'd bring it up specially from Cork, but this was another interpretation. He was a very early adopter of the idea of using it all year round. You'd never see it on a menu back then; it was a real Christmas-only thing in Cork, and not available at all in the rest of the country. I've tried it in Pepper with ordinary beef, but in The Market Bar I used spiced beef and it was much better.

Using only walnut oil for the vinaigrette would be too strong, so I just use olive oil and a little walnut oil to scent. This vinaigrette is really delicious so the recipe is more than you'll need for serving up this particular dish, allowing you to keep some over in the fridge to use for up to two weeks afterwards. Remember, the better quality the oils and vinegar, the better the dressing will be.

—Peter Clifford

Spiced beef should not just be served hot with the turkey as a Christmas food. The Cork delicacy, cut thin when cold, is our replacement for the Italian prosciutto.

—Michael Clifford

Ingredients

Dressing
1 sprig each, fresh thyme and
  rosemary
1 clove garlic
12 white peppercorns
1 tsp sea salt
150ml virgin olive
150ml vegetable oil
75ml walnut oil
125ml white wine vinegar
10ml lemon juice

Salad
200g mixed salad leaves
120g spiced beef, cooked
1 avocado, cut into cubes
100g Crozier Blue cheese,
  diced or crumbled
12 walnuts, roughly chopped

Method

For the dressing, put the herbs, garlic, salt and pepper into a storage jar. Combine all the liquids and pour them into the jar. Shake well.

For the salad, wash and spin the salad leaves. Thinly slice the spiced beef. Add the beef, avocado, cheese and walnuts to the salad leaves. Toss well.

To serve, add the vinaigrette and season to taste. Toss once more. Serve in a large salad bowl.

CURED SALMON AND CRAB SALAD WITH BUTTERMILK DRESSING, APPLE MERINGUE AND PEA MOUSSE

Serves 6 to 8

There are an awful lot more ingredients in this dish than would be in my dad's dishes, and some of the ingredients would seem totally crazy to him, but it's a cracking dish! It's lovely, light and summery. The apple breaks it down and the pea mousse is fresh, and good for the waistline, if you're worried about that. This recipe makes more mousse than you will need for this dish but you can use it up the next day: smeared on a cheesy omelette or a frittata for a quick, delicious snack with a bit of salad and some of my crusty, black olive bread or even added at the last minute to a 'green veg' soup. For the apple liquor, I've sometimes experimented with Mickey Finn's apple-flavoured whiskey, which is probably more at home on a shot tray in a club very late at night, but the flavour works really well in the meringue. Call it my twenty-first-century version of my dad's much-loved Madeira. I'll admit that this dish is a bit fussy, but it's definitely worth the effort.

—Peter Clifford

Ingredients

Cured Salmon
600g salmon fillet, skin on
15g sugar
15g sea salt
Zest of 1 lemon
1 pinch of black pepper

Pea Mousse
500ml chicken stock
250g peas
25g butter
3g gelatine sheet
100g whipped cream
1 tbsp sugar

Apple Meringue
50g egg whites
50g caster sugar
50g icing sugar, sieved
10ml apple brandy, Calvados
   or Mickey Finn's apple-
   flavoured

Apple Puree
6 dessert apples
30g butter
200ml apple juice

Crab Salad
300g crabmeat
2tbsp crème fraiche
Juice of half a lemon
1 tbsp chopped chives

Buttermilk Dressing
90ml buttermilk
30ml rice wine vinegar
1 shallot, finely chopped
1 tsp fresh dill
50ml extra-virgin olive oil

Method

Mix the sugar, salt, lemon zest and pepper in a blender. Place salmon in a bowl and pour this curing mixture over it. Leave for 8 hours in the fridge, turning once after 4 hours. Check that it has firmed up and the colour has changed slightly (compared to an un-cured piece). Rinse and pat it dry with a paper towel.

For the pea mousse, bring the chicken stock to the boil and then put it in a blender along with the peas, butter, sugar and seasoning, and whizz to a fine purée. Pass through a fine sieve. Soak the gelatine in cold water. Measure out 100g of the pea purée and heat gently until barely simmering. Remove from the heat and whisk in the gelatine. Add to the rest of the purée and leave to cool. Whip the cream until soft peaks form. Gently fold the cream into the pea purée, add salt and leave to set in the fridge.

For the apple meringue, whisk the egg whites until soft peaks form, and then start adding the caster sugar in a slow stream, whisking all the time. Then whisk in the sieved icing sugar and fold in the apple liquor. Place in a piping bag and pipe small meringues (the size of a €1 coin) at 2cm intervals onto a baking tray lined with greaseproof paper. Bake in a pre-heated 100° Celsius oven for 30 minutes or until the meringues are dry.

For the apple purée, peel and finely slice the apples, discarding the cores. Melt the butter in a pan until sizzling, add the apples and stir to coat in butter. Pour in 150ml apple juice, cover and simmer for 10 minutes, stirring occasionally. Add more apple juice if the pan begins to dry out. Cook until the apples have collapsed and become a 'fluffy' sauce. Transfer to a blender, blitz until smooth and pass through a sieve. Store in the fridge until required.

For the crab salad, mix the crabmeat, crème fraiche, lemon juice and chives lightly in a bowl with a spoon or fork until bound together. Season to taste. For the buttermilk dressing, blend the buttermilk, vinegar, shallot and dill in the blender. Slowly add the oil in a thin, continuous stream to make an emulsion, season with salt and pepper to taste, and store in the fridge.

There are no hard rules on how to serve to this, but you could use three portions of salmon and three portions of crème fraiche, dot all the other ingredients around and drizzle on the buttermilk dressing.

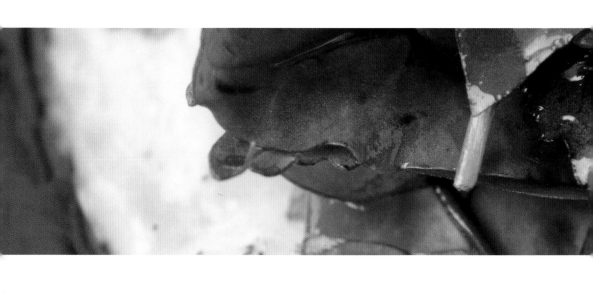

WARM SMOKED HADDOCK SALAD
SERVES 2

This was a recipe that my dad got from Vettard in Lyon and first introduced to his menu in Clifford's. I would have eaten it plenty of times before but the first time I cooked it was for this book. It is a very simple, lovely, summery dish that goes very well with a glass of wine. Definitely do not use dyed haddock. Get a piece of properly smoked haddock.

—Peter Clifford

Smoked fish used to be eaten in Ireland as a Lenten penance but it is wonderful raw material . . . For comfort eating among friends, you will find yourself returning again and again to this salad.

—Michael Clifford

INGREDIENTS

500g smoked haddock,
  finely sliced

60ml extra virgin olive oil

Juice of 1 lemon

2 tbsp dill, chopped

Assortment of crisp salad
  leaves

METHOD

Arrange the smoked haddock on a large plate. Mix 50ml olive oil and half the lemon juice and brush lightly on the haddock. Sprinkle on the dill and some milled pepper and place under the grill (or in the oven at 180° Celsius) for 3 to 4 minutes.

Toss the salad leaves in the rest of the olive oil and lemon juice and a little salt.

To serve, place the haddock in a fan shape in the centre of a large serving plate and arrange the salad leaves around the fish. Best eaten with a crunchy, fresh baguette.

FLAME-GRILLED MACKEREL, AVOCADO MOUSSE AND PICKLED VEGETABLES, WITH SOY AND CEP DRESSING

Serves 4

This is cured mackerel that is then flame-grilled to crisp it up. I'm always experimenting with ways of serving cured mackerel in this style. I love mackerel and could never tire of eating it. The trick is to get it as fresh as possible because it goes off so quickly. You can nearly see your face in that beautiful shiny skin when it's just out of the water.

—Peter Clifford

Ingredients

Cured Mackerel
2 mackerel, gutted, filleted,
  boned
15g sea salt
15g sugar
1 lemon, zested

Pickled Vegetables
10 radishes
1 cucumber
1 carrot
100ml water
100ml white wine vinegar
100ml white wine
50g caster sugar
20g coriander seeds
10 black peppercorns
3 star anise
1 sprig tarragon
1 sprig thyme

Avocado Mousse
500g avocados
250ml water
80g glucose syrup
10ml lemon juice

Soy and Cep Dressing
25g shallots, diced
130ml olive oil
50g button mushrooms, finely
  diced
2 sprigs thyme
10g soy sauce
50ml cep liquor

Method

To cure the mackerel, mix the salt, sugar, lemon zest and pepper in a blender. Rub all over the mackerel flesh and leave in a shallow tray for 2 hours in the fridge. Then remove the fish and rinse it and pat dry with paper towel.

To pickle the vegetables, thinly slice the radishes, cucumber and carrot. Bring the water, vinegar, white wine, sugar and spices to a gentle boil. Pour this on top of the vegetables and leave in the fridge. They will be ready to use after 1 hour, but if you want to store them for a few days, drain off the pickle juice and keep the pickled vegetables in a brine solution of 7 percent salt to water.

For the avocado mousse, dice the avocadoes and put them in the blender. Bring the water, glucose syrup and lemon juice to a boil and then pour into the blender. Blitz all the ingredients together and then pass them through a fine sieve. Put into a bowl and allow to set in the fridge.

For the soy and cep dressing, make the cep liquor by leaving 4 to 5 cep (porcini) mushrooms to steep for 25 minutes in 50ml boiling water. Then sweat the shallots and a pinch of salt in 30ml of the olive oil until lightly coloured. Add the mushrooms and thyme and sweat for a further 2 minutes. Add the soy sauce and reduce to nothing, then add the cep liquor and reduce by half. Place in the blender and blend to a fine purée. If you have access to fresh truffles, a slice or two added at this stage would change this very nice dressing into something truly magical. Warm 100ml of olive oil and add to the purée. Season and the pass through a fine sieve. Place into a plastic bottle and serve at room temperature.

To serve, place one piece of fish on each plate, drizzle the dressing around and place the pickled vegetables on top and all around.

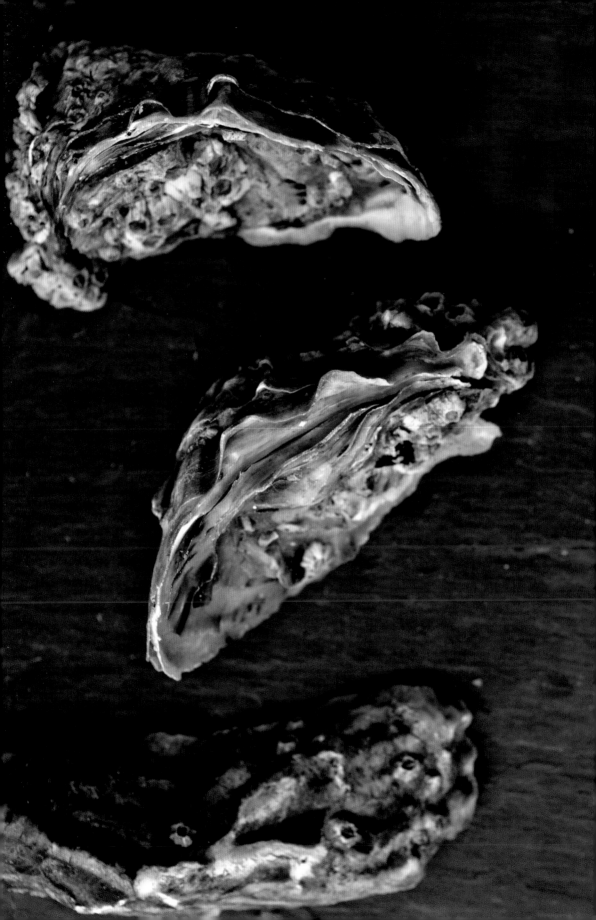

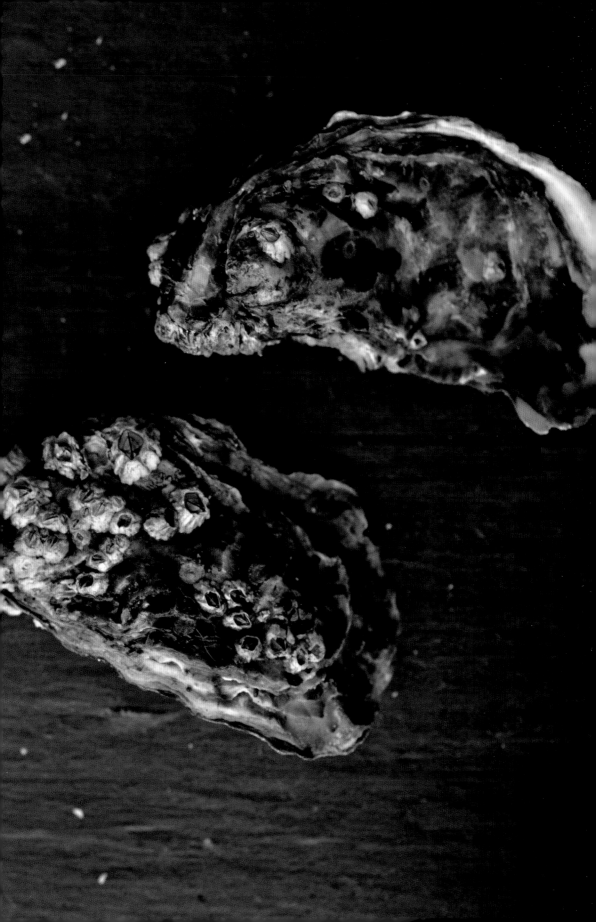

3

MAIN COURSES

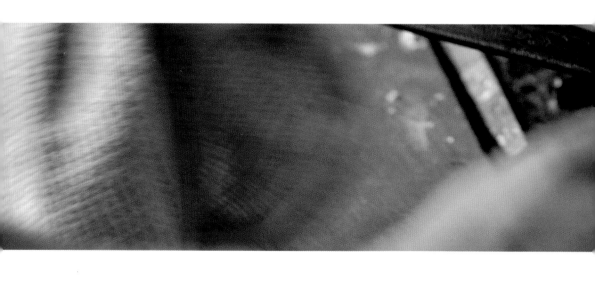

LAMBS' LIVER SAUTÉ WITH PORT AND GRAPES

SERVES 2

My dad had this as a starter in the Mardyke and used to serve it on a purée of white veg. It's a very quick and simple dish for home. It's healthy and very nice with a green salad and a bit of crusty white bread to mop up the sauce.

—Peter Clifford

INGREDIENTS

225g lambs' liver

25g butter

125ml veal stock (substitute lamb or chicken stock, if necessary)

Dash of port

75g grapes, deseeded and chopped

METHOD

Slice the liver widthways into small pieces, approximately 3cm across. Melt half the butter in a pan. Sauté the liver lightly. It should be still pink in the centre. Remove from the pan and keep warm. Add the stock and port to the pan and reduce slightly. In a separate pan, warm the grapes with the remaining butter. Season and taste. To serve, place the liver on the plate and pour the sauce around it. Add a spoonful of grapes to each plate.

LAMB SWEETBREADS WITH CELERIAC AND FENNEL
SERVES 4

This is one of my dad's dishes. He described it as 'an unusual and delicious starter'. With the whole revival in 'nose-to-tail' eating, he'd probably no longer call it unusual, but it is still delicious.

—Peter Clifford

Ingredients

375g lamb sweetbreads

125ml good lamb stock

1 to 2 potatoes

½ small celeriac, peeled and
  chopped into 2cm cubes

¼ fennel bulb, chopped finely

30ml cream

Knob of butter

15ml olive oil

Method

Soak the sweetbreads in cold salted water for 1 hour. Prepare a pot of boiling salted water and blanch the sweetbreads for 2 minutes. Remove the sweetbreads from the pot and refresh them under cold running water, which will cool them down so they stop cooking. Remove any membrane and gristle. Cut the sweetbreads in half, season and set aside.

Cook the celeriac in a little salted water until very tender, drain and purée with 10ml of cream. Set aside and keep warm. Put the lamb stock and chopped fennel in a pot, cook for 5 to 6 minutes and then liquidise. Return to pot and reheat with the knob of butter. Separately, cook the potatoes and purée them with 20ml of cream. Add the potato purée to the liquidised fennel and season to taste.

Now fry the sweetbreads quickly in olive oil until caramelised, about 4 to 5 minutes.

To serve, place some celeriac purée in the centre of a preheated plate. Spoon the fennel sauce around. Arrange the sweetbreads around a central nest of celeriac purée. Garnish with a little chopped tomato, if desired.

LEG OF LAMB WITH PEAR-AND-THYME SAUCE
SERVES 6 TO 8

My mother would actually use this recipe if she had guests over for lunch or at Easter. It's a very nice dish, one that I associate with home as much as any of the restaurants, a real family Sunday-dinner dish. It's delicious with baked creamed spinach.

—Peter Clifford

Ingredients

Lamb

1 leg of lamb
2 cloves of garlic, cut into slivers
1 sprig of fresh thyme
10ml olive oil
125ml water
1 onion, sliced
1 small pear
1 tsp honey

Sauce

125ml lamb stock
1 small pear, peeled and chopped
1 sprig of fresh thyme
4 crushed white peppercorns
1 tsp honey
1 tsp white wine vinegar
25g butter

Method

Preheat the oven to 180° Celsius. Prepare the leg of lamb for roasting by trimming off any excess fat and scoring little slits into the remaining fat. Insert garlic and thyme into these slits. Brush with olive oil. Place the joint in the roasting tin with the sliced onion and water. Cook for between 1 hour 20 minutes and 1 hour 40 minutes, according to taste. Top up the water during cooking if the roasting pan begins to dry out.

About 10 minutes before the lamb is fully cooked, peel and deseed the pear, and then liquidise or mash it with the honey. Remove the joint from the oven and deglaze the cooking pan with the honey-and-pear mixture. Drizzle the honey-and-pear juice from the cooking pan over the lamb, return to the oven and finish cooking. When the lamb is cooked to your liking, wrap it in foil and keep it warm. Remove the onion and any excess fat from the roasting tin. Keep the remaining juices for the sauce.

Place the lamb stock, pear, thyme, peppercorns, honey and vinegar in a saucepan. Cook gently for about 1 minute. Pass through a fine sieve. Return the liquid to the saucepan with the juices from the roasting tin and reheat.

To serve, carve the lamb and then reheat the sauce and quickly stir in the butter. Put a little sauce over each serving of lamb.

LOIN OF SPRING LAMB WITH SWEETBREAD-AND-KIDNEY MOUSSE, MINT AND SORREL

SERVES 4

The first time my dad did this dish was in the Arbutus Lodge, and he also did it in White's on the Green. It was a big favourite with the customers, one he loved to cook. He even used it as his winning entry in a lamb-cooking competition. Using ginger in this dish seems a funny one to me but he used it a lot – perhaps because it was a fresh 'spice' that was both obtainable and relatively easy to store for a long time, back in a time when more exotic produce was much harder to source.

—Peter Clifford

Ingredients

1 loin of spring lamb
1 clove garlic
1 sprig rosemary
Mousse

100g lamb sweetbreads
100g lamb kidneys
2 lamb fillets
1 egg white
100ml cream
1 tsp ginger, finely chopped

Sauce
300ml lamb (or veal) stock
250ml white wine
100ml cream
10g butter
1 tsp mint leaves, chopped
½ tsp sorrel leaves, chopped

Method

To make the mousse, leave the sweetbreads under cold running water for 20 minutes, transfer to a saucepan, cover with salted cold water, bring to the boil and simmer for 10 minutes. Remove from the water and refresh under cold running water, to cool the sweetbreads and stop them from cooking further. Remove any membrane and gristle, cut the sweetbreads into small pieces, season and set aside.

Next, remove fat and membrane from the kidneys, cut them into small pieces, season and set aside. Liquidise the lamb fillets with the egg whites, chill for half an hour, add cream and seasoning and pass through a sieve. Heat a pan with some olive oil and butter, add the ginger, kidneys and sweetbreads and toss them over a high heat to brown/caramelise them. Transfer the ginger, kidneys and sweetbreads from the pan to a dish and mix them with the mousse made from the fillet.

Make an incision along the top of the loin, cutting about two-thirds of the way down into the meat to form a 'purse' and taking care not to cut through to the other side, or the mousse will escape during cooking. Spoon the mousse into the cavity and then tie the loin closed carefully with string to fully enclose the mousse. Heat some cooking oil in a pan, add a clove of garlic and a sprig of rosemary and brown the loin on all sides. Transfer to an oven preheated to 180° Celsius. If you want it rare, cook for 20 minutes per kilogram plus 15 minutes.

To make the sauce, pour the stock and white wine into a saucepan and cook until reduced by half. Add the cream and reduce again by half. Whisk in the butter and check the seasoning. Add the chopped mint and sorrel leaves at the very end. Taste again to check the seasoning. Slice the lamb, arrange nicely on plates and surround with the sauce.

CLIFFORD'S LAMB STEW
SERVES 4 TO 6

Dad took a very serious approach to what many people might think of as tired old Irish standard dishes. If he was going to do a stew, it would have to be the very best one possible, and he was enormously proud of his lamb stew. This recipe was adapted by Bord Bia to become the 'definitive modern Irish Stew' whenever they were showcasing Ireland and its produce.

—Peter Clifford

INGREDIENTS

1 shoulder of lamb, boned by the butcher

1 bone from the shoulder of lamb, chopped

1l water

4 potatoes, chopped

2 carrots, chopped

2 small white turnips, chopped

1 onion, chopped

1 leek, finely sliced

50g green cabbage, finely shredded

125ml cream

Worcestershire sauce

1 tbsp chopped parsley

METHOD

Cut the lamb into cubes and place in a large pot. Cover with cold water. Bring to the boil. Drain, rinse lamb and place in a clean pot with the bones. Cover with approximately 1l water. Add 2 potatoes, 1 carrot, 1 turnip, onion and leek, setting aside the remaining potatoes, carrot, turnip and cabbage. Cover the pot and cook gently for approximately 1 hour, or until the meat is tender. Remove the meat and set it aside.

Discard the bones. Liquidise the cooked vegetables and liquid, and return to the pot. Add the cream, Worcestershire sauce and chopped parsley. Neatly chop the remaining 2 potatoes, carrot and turnip, and blanch in boiling salted water for 4 minutes. Add the cabbage and continue to cook for another 3 to 4 minutes or until tender.

Transfer the blanched vegetables and meat into the main pot. Taste for seasoning. Serve in warm, deep plates with extra chopped parsley and freshly made wholemeal bread.

ROAST BEEF, PLAIN AND SIMPLE

This is a bit of a manifesto from dad. It might seem like old hat but this is one of the classic dishes and you either get it right or you get it wrong. He was a great believer that the very best dishes start with the very best ingredients.

—Peter Clifford

At its best, there is no dish equal to roast beef. To get the best results, start with the correct cut. The very best would be the short sirloin (T-bone) left in the piece. You have to be prepared to buy a decent-sized piece, 2kg to 2½kg on the bone. The next best is the rib roast, also left on the bone. For this you will need a double rib as a single one is too thin. It looks the same as a sirloin but without the undercut (fillet). It is best to buy and cook the joint on the bone. The bone provides good flavour and it is also a good conductor of heat inside the joint, thus cooking the meat more evenly and with less loss of juice. However, if you prefer, both sirloin and rib roasts can be boned and rolled. If you feel that your family is too small for a large joint, remember, good roast beef is delicious cold with chutney and baked potatoes or in salads. It is also very useful for nutritious lunch boxes during the week. More economical and very lean are the cuts from the round. These need slower roasting but they do have a good flavour.

—Michael Clifford

METHOD

Remove the joint from the fridge 1 hour before cooking. Dust any exposed fat with a mixture of dry mustard and freshly ground black pepper. Preheat the oven to 200° Celsius. Place the meat on a rack (if available) in the roasting tin.

Start by giving the joint 20 minutes in the hot oven. Reduce the heat to 170° Celsius and allow 15 minutes per 500g for rare, 20 minutes for medium and 30 minutes for well-done. If you want very accurate results, use a meat thermometer.

Plan the meal so that the joint is allowed to 'relax' for about 30 minutes before it is served. This will make the carving easier and it will give you a chance to increase the oven heat to crisp roast potatoes, if you're serving them.

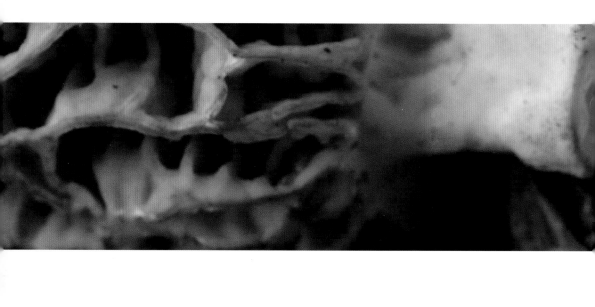

WINE-AND-MUSHROOM SAUCE TO SERVE WITH PRIME RIB OR BEEF

This is a real old-school sauce, and there's nothing at all wrong with that. I get nostalgic just thinking about it.

—Peter Clifford

INGREDIENTS

15g butter

1 shallot, finely chopped

8 large oyster mushrooms,
  very finely chopped

125ml cream

125ml beef stock

20ml brandy

Knob of butter

METHOD

Melt the 15g of butter in a small pan and sauté the shallot in it. Add the mushrooms, cream, stock and brandy. Bring to a boil and cook until the sauce has reduced by half and thickened. Whisk in a knob of butter and season. To serve, carve the beef and pour a little sauce over each serving.

CHICKEN RAVIOLI IN MILLEENS CHEESE SAUCE, WITH APPLE AND WALNUTS

SERVES 6

This is my take on my dad's signature dish of chicken quenelles and has always been one of the most popular dishes on my menus.

—Peter Clifford

Ingredients

Pasta
200g 00 flour
2 whole eggs
5ml olive oil
Pinch of salt

Chicken Mousse
300g uncooked chicken
   breast
Squeeze of lemon juice
1 egg white
250ml cream
Pinch of salt

Milleens Cheese Sauce
1 small shallot, diced
1 knob of butter
100ml white wine
250ml chicken stock
150ml fresh cream
15g Milleens cheese, rind
   removed, diced

Garnish
1 dessert apple
12 walnuts

Method

To make the pasta, place the flour, eggs, olive oil and salt in a blender and pulse until the mixture is fully combined, about 30 seconds. Place onto a floured worktop, knead the mixture for 7 to 8 minutes and then place in the fridge for 30 minutes. When chilled, cut into 4 or 5 portions and roll the pasta through your pasta machine according to the manufacturer's instructions, starting at the largest setting and working your way down to the smallest. Set the finished long sheets aside.

To make the chicken mousse, roughly chop the chicken and place it in the blender with the lemon juice and egg white. Blitz for 1 minute and then slowly add the cream. Blitz again until the mixture is very smooth. Season with salt. Place the mixture in a bowl and let it rest in the fridge until it cools and firms up, about 30 minutes.

To make the sauce, sweat the shallot in the butter. Add the white wine and chicken stock and reduce by half. Add the cream and reduce until slightly thickened. Whisk in the Milleens cheese and pass through a fine sieve. Adjust salt to taste.

To make the ravioli, take 1 sheet of pasta and dot heaped tablespoons of the chilled chicken mousse along an imaginary line, just off centre, at regular intervals, allowing 7 to 8 centimetres between each spoonful. Place a small cube of Milleens cheese in the centre of each spoonful. Then fold the sheet over to completely enclose the spoonfuls of chicken mousse. Gently press down all around each spoonful to ensure that no air is trapped inside. Cut out each one with a circle cutter (about 10cm in diameter) and leave to rest.

Prepare the garnish by finely dicing the apple or cutting it into julienne strips (long 'matchsticks'). Put these in water with a little lemon juice to keep them from discolouring. Roast the walnuts in the oven at 180° Celsius for 3 to 4 minutes and then roughly chop them.

Blanch the ravioli in boiling salted water for 8 minutes or until cooked. If you have a food probe or thermometer, the mousse inside needs to reach 73° Celsius. Place the ravioli in a warm bowl, spoon the Milleens cheese sauce on top and garnish with apples and walnuts.

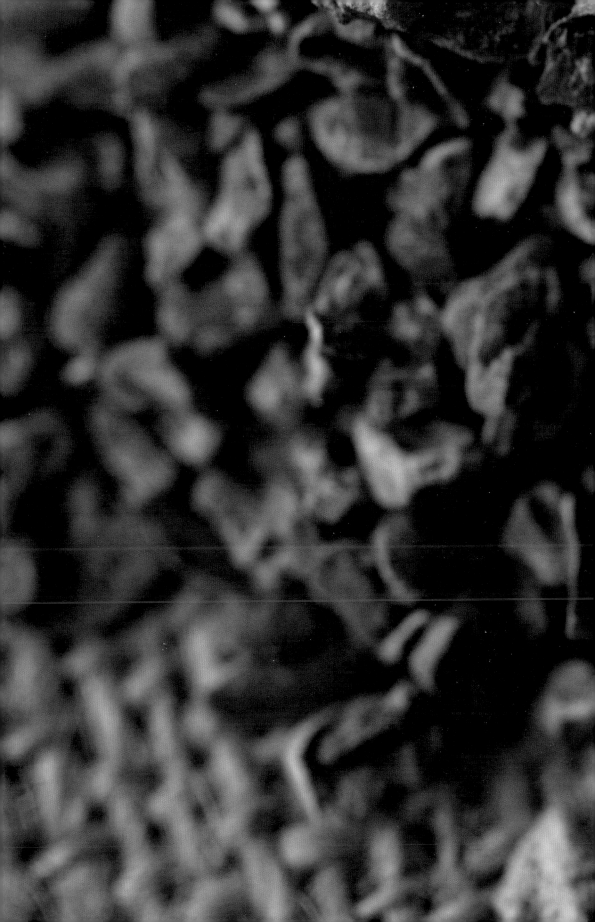

RILLETTE OF DUCK AND PORK
SERVES 6 TO 8

This would have been a classic bistro dish in Cork. It is a lovely picnic dish with a nice relish, some green salad and a crunchy baguette. It also makes for a great canapé or appetiser that can be prepared well in advance and served on toast with drinks.

—Peter Clifford

INGREDIENTS

1kg pork fat

400g duck fat

1.5kg duck legs

350g pork fillet

1 bottle white wine

150ml water

1 whole carrot

1 small onion, cut into quarters

2 cloves of garlic

10g green peppercorns, crushed

1 bunch of tied herbs (thyme, sage, parsley)

1 tbsp sea salt

METHOD

Place the duck and pork fat in a deep roasting pan and melt in the oven at 160° Celsius. Pass through a sieve into a clean pan, cool until lukewarm and add the duck legs, pork fillet, white wine, water, carrot, onion, garlic, peppercorns, herbs and salt, completely immersing the duck legs and pork. Simmer in oven for 1 hour. Drain off the remaining liquid and remove the herbs and vegetables. Remove the bones from the duck legs and flake the meat into small pieces. Do the same with the pork fillet. Mix the meat together and place in a 450g earthenware dish or loaf tin lined with cling film, with a weight on top to compress. Store in the fridge for 24 hours, slice and serve at room temperature.

CLIFFORD'S GAME PIE
SERVES 4

This dish combined my dad's love of shooting and game. In season, he always had this one on in the restaurant. I've eaten it loads of times and I always put it on in game-season as well. This could be considered one of his fundamental recipes – a don't-leave-home-without-it recipe – and is as good as any for giving an idea of the man through his food. Use any wild gamebird available: the more the merrier, but it's still a great dish with just one or two birds. I've served it with prunes macerated in port and star anise and a bit of braised red cabbage and chestnuts. I've never had the patience to wait, but I've a feeling it would also be good eaten cold as a winter picnic lunch.

—Peter Clifford

Ingredients

2 shallots, sliced
1 clove garlic, crushed
2 sprigs thyme
25g butter
250g game meat, finely sliced
1 large Rooster potato, grated
280g puff-pastry sheet
125ml fresh cream
2 tbsp milk
1 egg

Method

Sauté shallots, crushed garlic and thyme in butter. Mix with the finely sliced game meat, add grated potato and season with salt and pepper. Line the base of a shallow baking dish with pastry, place the filling on top, cover with the rest of the pastry and secure the edges. Brush the pastry with an egg wash made by beating together the milk and egg, and cut a 1cm circular hole in the centre of the pie to act as a 'chimney' for steam. Cook for 20 minutes at 185° Celsius. Meanwhile, reduce the cream by half. Remove the pie from the oven, pour the reduced cream into the hole, cook for a further 5 minutes and then serve.

BRACE OF QUAIL WITH MANGO-AND-GINGER SAUCE

SERVES 2

Here's the ginger again, and also mango, a fruit my dad was very fond of using, which was especially exotic in Ireland back in the '80s and '90s. I've cooked this dish and it makes for a very nice starter; a fresh, clean take on serving quail.

—Peter Clifford

INGREDIENTS

4 quail

1 tbsp sunflower oil

2 cloves garlic

1 sprig thyme

30ml dry white wine

200ml water

1 mango

10g to 15g ginger, finely
  diced

1 knob of butter

METHOD

Season the quail and place it in a hot ovenproof pan with the oil, garlic and thyme. Brown the quail on both sides and transfer the pan to a medium oven, 170° Celsius. Cook for only 4 minutes, as the quail is a delicate bird and the flesh should remain pink. Place the quail on a chopping board and remove the legs and breasts. Set them aside and keep them warm.

To make the sauce, roughly chop the remaining quail bones, place in a saucepan with cooking juices from roasting pan and add the white wine and water. Cook until reduced by half. Pass through a sieve. Purée the mango and ginger, add to the quail stock, season to taste and add a knob of butter.

To serve, place the quail legs and breasts on plates, pour mango-and-ginger sauce around and garnish with finely sliced mango.

STEW OF CLONAKILTY BLACKPUDDING WITH FLAGEOLET BEANS AND HOME-MADE SAUSAGES

SERVES 4

Here's another classic from the bistro, one I've also served up in the gastro-bar in Pepper. It's a serious winter dish, a sort of Ireland-meets-France (or Spain) in the pot, but deeply comforting, as all good stews are.

—Peter Clifford

INGREDIENTS

300g flageolet beans

1 medium onion, diced

2 cloves garlic, crushed

1 knob of butter

25g smoked bacon lardons

1l chicken stock

1 bunch of tied herbs (sage, thyme, parsley, bay leaf)

1 glass white wine

200g tinned plum tomatoes

1 ring of Clonakilty Blackpudding, sliced

6 home-made pork sausages

1 tbsp chopped flat-leaf parsley

METHOD

Soak the flageolet beans for 6 to 8 hours in advance of cooking. Wash very well before use. Sweat the onions and garlic in the knob of butter. Add the bacon and flageolet beans, and cook for 3 to 4 minutes, stirring regularly, then add the chicken stock, herbs, wine and tomatoes. Bring to the boil and simmer for 1.5 hours or until the beans are cooked. In a separate pan, fry the black pudding and sausages. Pour the bean stew into a serving dish and place the black pudding and sausages on top. Garnish with the chopped flat-leaf parsley and serve with a good baguette to mop up the sauce.

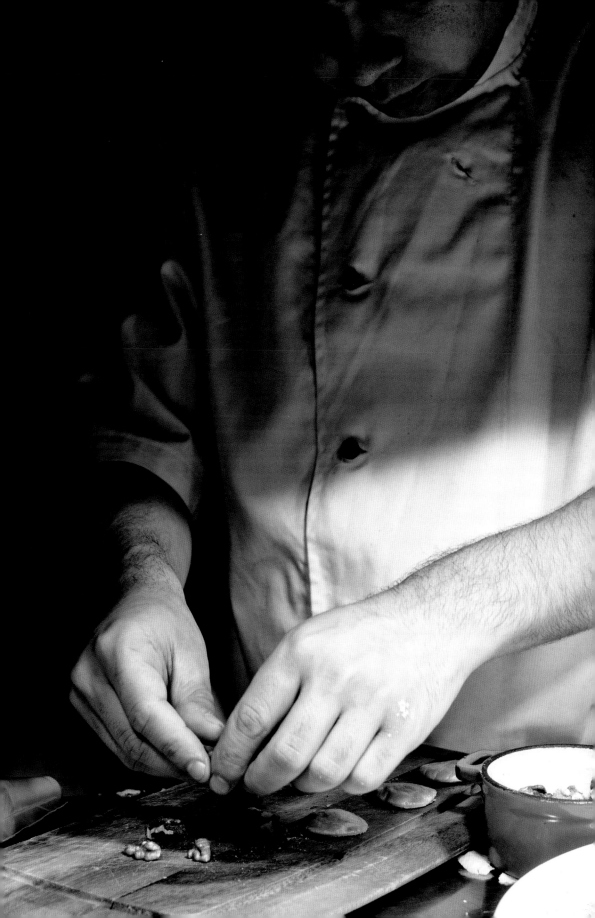

BROCCOLI 'COUSCOUS' WITH YOGURT *ESPUMA*

SERVES 4

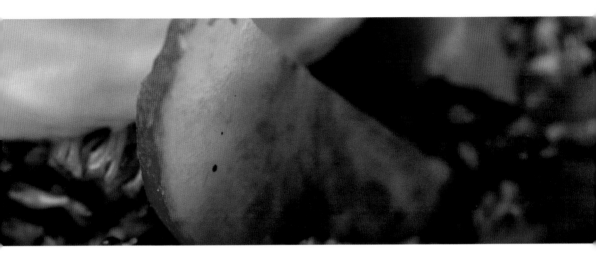

This recipe calls for the use of a rather 'cheffy' piece of kit – a cream gun or cream whipper – but the result is excellent. If you don't have a cream gun, I have offered a very simple alternative recipe below, mixing cream and yoghurt. I know which one my dad would probably have opted for!

—Peter Clifford

INGREDIENTS

Broccoli 'Couscous'
1 head of broccoli
1 banana shallot
1 tbsp chopped chives
200ml rapeseed oil
Juice of one lemon
50g flaked almonds,
  toasted

'Cheffy' Yogurt Espuma
1 gelatine sheet
30ml water
300g natural yogurt
Juice of half a lemon

Simple Yogurt Espuma
200ml cream
100ml natural yoghurt
Juice of half a lemon

Garnish
Flat-leaf parsley
Coriander
Baby rocket
Edible flowers
1 blood orange,
  segmented

METHOD

Toast the flaked almonds on a tray in a medium-hot oven for a couple of minutes, checking *very* regularly and turning once. Put the almonds to one side.

Finely chop the broccoli until it resembles couscous. Finely chop the shallot and chives and add to the broccoli. Mix the oil and lemon juice, add to the vegetables and leave to marinate for 20 minutes. Season with salt.

To make the 'cheffy' yogurt *espuma*, soak the gelatine leaf in cold water. Separately, place 30ml of water in the pot, bring to a simmer and then remove from the heat. Squeeze out the gelatine to remove any excess water and whisk it into the hot water until fully dissolved. Place the yogurt in a bowl, add the lemon juice and gelatine water, and whisk until all the ingredients are fully incorporated. Place this mix in a cream gun, charge with gas canisters and shake for 1 minute. Place in the fridge until ready to serve.

To make the simple yogurt *espuma*, whisk the cream until whipped. Separately, whisk the lemon juice into the yoghurt. Fold the yogurt mixture gently into the whipped cream.

To serve, first mix the almonds into the broccoli 'couscous'. (If you add them any earlier, they will take on liquid and soften, losing their 'bite'.) Then place the 'couscous' in a bowl and gently place some yoghurt *espuma* on top. Garnish with chopped herbs and orange.

POACHED EGG ON A BED OF SPINACH WITH NUTS AND GRAPES

Serves 4

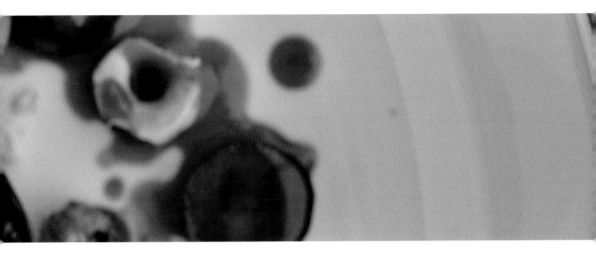

This is my dad's recipe and would have been a staple in Clifford's in Cork. It was inspired by a simple dish he saw in a Michelin three-star restaurant in the south of France. This dish could also be served with a very simple lemon-butter sauce.

—Peter Clifford

INGREDIENTS

4 free-range eggs

100ml chicken stock

50g assorted nuts (hazelnuts,
  walnuts, almonds, pine nuts)

20 green grapes, halved
  and deseeded

10ml port

25g butter

20ml olive oil

250g fresh spinach

1 pinch nutmeg

METHOD

Poach the eggs in a pan of simmering salted water. Set aside and keep warm. Put the chicken stock into a small pot. Add the nuts and the grapes, bring to the boil and reduce for 1 minute. Add the port and whisk in the butter.

Heat the olive oil in a moderate-to-hot pan and add the spinach leaves (leave stalks on baby spinach, remove stalks from older spinach), tossing constantly until they are tender – barely a minute. Season with salt, pepper and nutmeg.

To serve, place the spinach in the centre of the plate. With a spoon, place nuts and grapes on and around the spinach. Pour the sauce all over and place the egg on top.

LASAGNE OF TURBOT IN A LIGHT DIJON SAUCE
SERVES 2

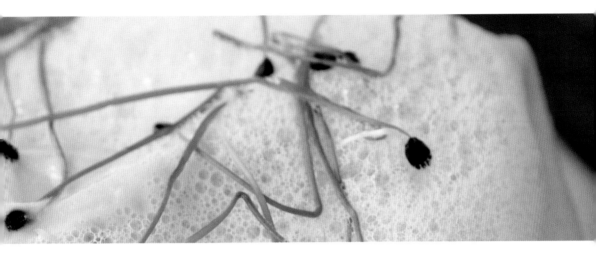

A nice lunch or brunch dish, this one is very simple. All you need is a good piece of turbot. If you have that, it speaks for itself. This dish serves two people so it also makes for a very impressive date-night dish, and, because so much preparation can be done in advance and the actual cooking is simple and quick, it allows you plenty of time to do a spot of romancing.

—Peter Clifford

INGREDIENTS

Dijon Sauce
1 shallot, diced
1 garlic clove, diced
30g butter
50ml white wine
50ml white wine vinegar
200ml cream
1 tbsp Dijon mustard
10ml lemon juice

Pasta
200g 00 flour
2 whole eggs
5ml olive oil
Pinch of salt

Turbot
2 fillets of fresh turbot
10ml olive oil
Chives, to garnish

METHOD

To make the Dijon sauce, in a pot, sauté the shallot and garlic in 10g of the butter for 1 minute, stirring continuously. Add the vinegar and white wine and reduce by half. Add the cream and simmer until it has reduced by half. Pass this mixture through a sieve and place in a clean pot. Bring back to the boil and whisk in the mustard, the remaining butter and the lemon juice. Season with salt.

To make the pasta, place all the ingredients in a blender and pulse until the mixture is fully combined, about 30 seconds. Place onto a floured work surface, knead the mixture for 7 to 8 minutes and place in fridge for 30 minutes. When chilled, roll the pasta through your pasta machine according to the manufacturer's instructions, starting at the largest setting and working your way down to the smallest. You will be left with long, narrow sheets. Cut these into 15cm squares. Just before cooking the turbot, cook the pasta squares in boiling, salted water for about 3 to 4 minutes (until al dente), and keep them warm.

Cut each turbot fillet into 4 equal pieces. Season and pan-fry quickly – approximately 1 to 2 minutes on each side – until the fish firms up and becomes nice and golden-brown. To serve, place a pasta square on the bottom of the bowl, place a piece of turbot on top and cover with sauce. Repeat this process three more times, layering the turbot, pasta, and sauce. Garnish with some chives.

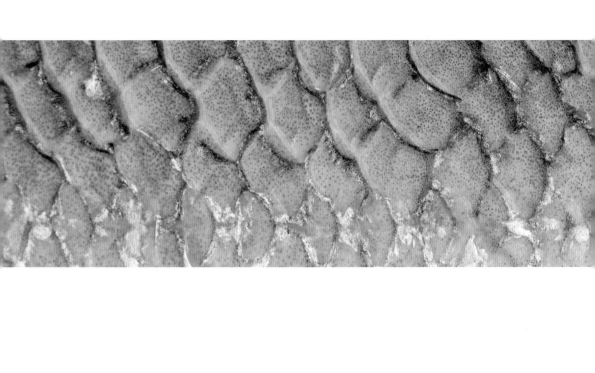

BAKED COD WITH COURGETTE AND PARMESAN CHEESE

Serves 4

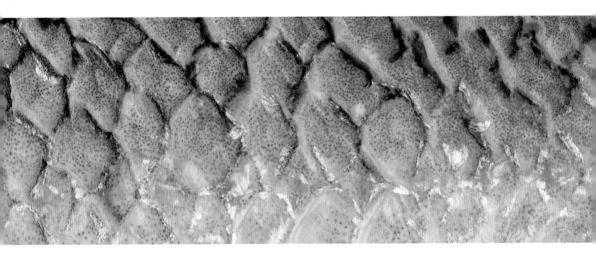

This is a dish from the bistro book – a very simple, very tasty and very quick dish. My sister Laura won the Young Chef of the Year competition the year after me and this is the dish she cooked. My dad used to do it as a demo dish.

—Peter Clifford

INGREDIENTS

600g fresh cod

50g fresh Parmesan cheese, grated

1 courgette

Squeeze of lemon juice

Olive oil, to brush

1 ripe tomato, peeled, deseeded and chopped

METHOD

Cut the cod into four pieces of about 150g each. Season with salt and pepper and lemon juice, brush with olive oil. Slice the courgette thinly and blanch for 2 minutes in boiling salted water. Arrange the courgette slices neatly on top of the pieces of fresh cod. Place some chopped tomato in the centre of each piece of fish, on top of the courgette slices, and sprinkle Parmesan cheese all over. Place on a buttered baking tray, cook in the oven at 160° Celsius for 15 minutes and then let rest in a warm place. Whip up a quick sauce to serve with the fish by heating the cooking juices in a small pot, whisking in a knob of butter and a squeeze of lemon juice and seasoning to taste.

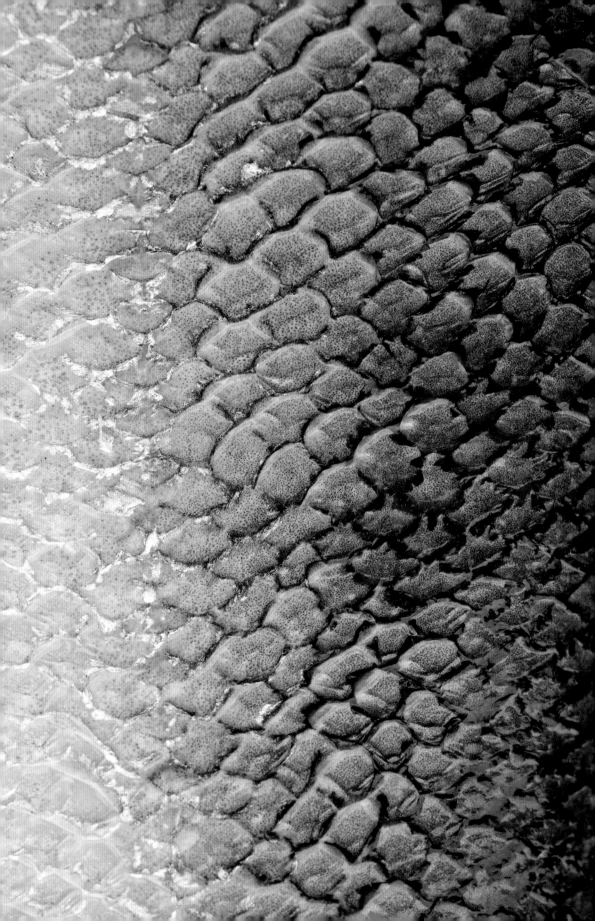

ESCALOPE OF SALMON IN WATERCRESS SAUCE
Serves 4

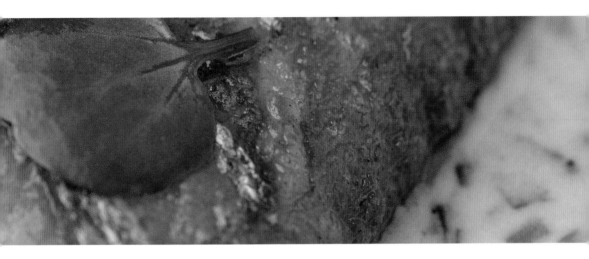

A simple dish, inspired by my dad's spell at the legendary Troisgros brothers' restaurant, in France, back in a time when a Teflon non-stick pan was a revolutionary new piece of kitchen kit. A lovely, simple summer dish, good with a crisp white wine – ideally the same wine as used to make the dish. At the Troisgros brothers' restaurant, they used sorrel instead of watercress for this dish.

—Peter Clifford

INGREDIENTS

100ml fish stock

100ml white wine

Dash of dry vermouth

1 shallot, finely chopped

125ml cream

100g watercress, chopped

25g unsalted butter

10ml lemon juice

Salt and freshly ground black
  pepper

1kg salmon, middle cut

METHOD

Put the fish stock, wine, vermouth and shallot in a pan over the heat and reduce by half. Add the cream and boil until the sauce has slightly thickened. Set aside four sprigs of watercress for garnish and finely chop the remainder. Add the watercress, butter and lemon juice to the pan. Season to taste and remove from the heat.

Remove all the bones from the salmon. Cut into 4 pieces, wrap loosely in cling film and flatten gently into an even thickness with a rolling pin. Remove cling film. Heat a non-stick pan without fat and season these escalopes. Put the escalopes into an extremely hot pan for 25 seconds before turning and cooking the other side for a further 20 to 25 seconds. It's better to undercook the salmon than to overcook it.

Spoon sauce over 4 large, preheated plates. Place a piece of salmon on top of the sauce on each plate. Garnish the salmon with sprigs of watercress.

PAN-FRIED SCALLOPS WITH FRIED EGG, BRIOCHE, MUSHROOMS AND BEURRE BLANC
Serves 2

This is another very popular dish from my repertoire, one I created in Pepper. It is a wonderful dish to eat and for some reason reminds me of the style of dish my dad would cook, maybe in the bistro! Joe McNamee loved it as well.

—Peter Clifford

Ingredients

Beurre Blanc

1 shallot, finely chopped

50ml white wine vinegar

50ml white wine

50ml water

120g cold unsalted butter,
  cut into small chunks

*Brioche, Mushrooms, Eggs
  and Scallops*

1 slice brioche, diced into
  croutons

100g wild mushrooms

30g butter

10ml sunflower oil

2 free-range eggs

6 fresh scallops with coral
  removed

10ml olive oil

10ml lemon juice

Method

Start by making the beurre blanc. Place the shallot, vinegar, wine and water into a saucepan over a moderate heat. Reduce until almost no liquid remains. Turn the heat down to a low setting, and whisk in the butter one piece at a time, allowing each piece to melt before adding the next. It is a good idea to take the pan away from the heat for a few seconds now and then to let it cool a little. Once all the butter has been used, the sauce should be pale and have a thin, custard-like consistency. Keep the sauce warm.

Crisp the brioche croutons under a moderate grill until golden-brown all over. Remove from the oven and place in an airtight container until required. Sauté the mushrooms with 10g of the butter in a moderate-to-hot pan for 1 minute. Season with salt and keep warm. Heat the sunflower oil in a moderate pan and gently fry the eggs until the whites are fully set.

Season the scallops with salt and cook in a very hot pan with the olive oil for 40 seconds on one side and then add the butter and cook for a further 20 seconds or until they turn nut brown. Then add the lemon juice, turn the scallops and remove them from the heat immediately so that they finish cooking on the residual heat.

To serve, place the egg in the middle of a warm plate and place three scallops around it. Evenly scatter the mushrooms around and place the brioche croutons on top. Drizzle with the sauce.

SEARED SCALLOPS AND TAGLIATELLE IN CARBONARA SAUCE WITH FRESH TRUFFLES

SERVES 2

This was always on the menu in Pepper, a signature dish that was extremely popular and went down very well when I demonstrated it at the Dublin Bay Prawn Festival, in Howth, County Dublin.

—Peter Clifford

INGREDIENTS

Sauce
1 medium onion, finely diced
2 cloves garlic, crushed
1 sprig thyme
50g pancetta, finely diced
10ml cooking oil
50ml white wine
500ml cream
15g Parmesan cheese, grated

Pasta
200g 00 flour
2 whole eggs
5ml olive oil
Pinch of salt

Scallops
6 scallops, very fresh, with
  coral removed
10ml olive oil
20g butter
10ml lemon juice

METHOD

To make the sauce, sauté the onion, garlic, thyme and pancetta in cooking oil in a fairly hot saucepan for 5 minutes, stirring regularly to ensure it doesn't burn. Add white wine and reduce by half, add cream and bring to a boil, then reduce to a simmer for 10 minutes. Pass sauce through a fine sieve, whisk in the cheese and season with salt and pepper to taste.

To make the pasta, place the flour, eggs, olive oil and salt into a blender and pulse until the mixture is fully combined, about 30 seconds. Place onto a floured work surface, knead for 7 to 8 minutes and place in the fridge for 30 minutes. When chilled, make tagliatelle according to the pasta-machine instructions and leave the pasta to dry at room temperature for at least 15 minutes.

Place the pasta in a large pot of boiling salted water for 3 to 4 minutes, until tender but still retaining a nice al dente bite. Season the scallops with salt and cook in a very hot pan with the olive oil for 40 seconds on one side and then add the butter and cook for a further 20 seconds, or until turning nut brown, then add the lemon juice, turn the scallops, remove from the heat immediately and finish cooking with the residual heat. Place cooked pasta in a bowl and place scallops on top. Spoon the sauce around. If you're lucky enough to have some to hand, grate some fresh truffle on top.

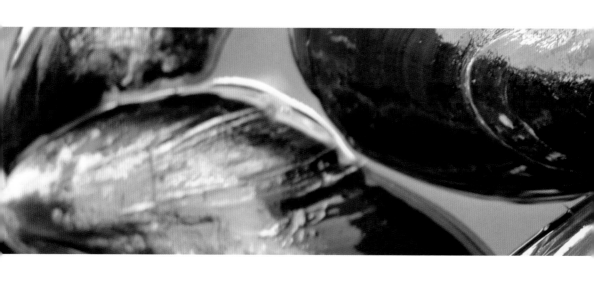

STEAMED MUSSELS AND CLAMS, SCENTED WITH LEMONGRASS

Serves 6

This is a dish from the bistro days. Lemongrass at the time must have seemed very exotic indeed to Irish palates. Though you can get it easily enough in the supermarkets now, the quality is not necessarily always that great. Give it a good bashing before using it, to release more flavour.

—Peter Clifford

INGREDIENTS

1.5kg mussels

1kg clams

150ml white wine

150ml water

½ lemon, sliced

½ onion, diced

1 stick lemongrass

1 bay leaf

1 bunch parsley, leaves
  chopped, stalks reserved

250ml cream

1 tsp *beurre manié*

METHOD

Wash the mussels and clams well, making sure to remove beards from the mussels. Place the wine, water, lemon, onion, lemongrass, bay leaf and parsley stalks into a large pot. Steam mussels and clams in this liquid for 2 or 3 minutes, until the shells are just open. Remove the shellfish and place them in a serving dish large enough to accommodate them all.

Pass the cooking juices through a fine sieve into a small saucepan. Reduce by a quarter, add the cream, bring to a boil and whisk in the *beurre manié*. Add the chopped parsley leaves, pour the sauce over the shellfish and serve.

Note: *beurre manié* is equal parts flour and butter mixed together into a dough. Store it in the fridge wrapped in cling film for up to a week. You can also drop little knobs of it into soups, stews and casseroles near the end of the cooking process to thicken them up.

LOBSTER BURGER WITH AVOCADO MOUSSE

Serves 2

This is nice with a fresh salad but to really do it justice, it is best served with lovely home-made chips and chilled, dry white wine. This is one of my simpler recipes and it is very popular with the general public and critics alike, a real summertime smash.

—Peter Clifford

INGREDIENTS

Avocado Mousse
500g avocado flesh
230ml water
80g glucose syrup
10ml lemon juice

Lobster Burger
100ml water
50g butter
1 lobster, cooked and shelled
2 burger buns (brioche, if
  possible)
1 pinch of Maldon sea salt
10 walnuts, roasted
1 apple
6 leaves of baby gem lettuce

METHOD

To make the avocado mousse, blitz the avocado, water, glucose syrup and lemon juice in a blender until smooth. Scrape the mixture into a bowl, check and adjust the seasoning to suit, cover the bowl in cling film and place it in the fridge until required.

To prepare the lobster, warm the water and butter in a pot. Slice the lobster tail meat in half, then place with the meat from the two claws in the pot of warmed water and butter. Slowly heat the lobster until it's just hot. Remember, it's already cooked – we just want to reheat it. Remove from the water and keep it in a warm place.

Peel and core the apple. Slice it into julienne strips ('matchsticks') and store these in a bowl of water and lemon juice to keep them from discolouring. Roast the walnuts on a tray in a 180° Celsius oven for 3 to 4 minutes.

To build the burger, lightly toast the two halves of your burger bun under the grill. Spread a bit of the avocado mousse on each bun, place one piece of tail meat and one piece of claw meat on the bottom of the bun, and sprinkle with sea salt.

Place the walnuts and apples on the lobster meat and place 3 leaves of lettuce on top. Close with the top half of the bun.

LOBSTER BAVAROIS

SERVES 4 TO 6

This was a signature dish from dad's days in White's on the Green. It would have come from the Troisgros brothers or the Roux brothers, and been picked up and adapted on one his *stages*. I've done it in the Market Bar; it's a great dish.

—Peter Clifford

Ingredients

Meat of 2 fresh, uncooked
  lobsters

6 to 8 prawns

2 egg whites

Sauce

6 tbsp good-quality vegetable
  oil

Shell of 1 lobster

Shells of 6 to 8 prawns

2 medium carrots, peeled

½ large onion, peeled and
  finely diced

1 clove garlic, crushed

1 small *bouquet garni*
  (thyme, parsley stalks,
  stick of celery, bay leaf)

3 tbsp brandy

4 tbsp port

250ml dry white wine

3 tbsp tomato purée

400ml double cream

1 tsp chopped tarragon,
  preferably fresh

Method

Heat the oil in a sauté pan, add the lobster shells and prawn shells and cook, covered, for 5 minutes on medium heat. Then remove the shells and put in the mortar and pound roughly (or use a food processor) and put them back in the pan. Add the carrots and onions and sweat together with the garlic and *bouquet garni*. Do not let them brown.

Add brandy and port, cover the pan and boil until reduced by half. Add white wine, tomato purée, salt and pepper. Boil for about 10 minutes, until reduced by a third. Add cream and tarragon and simmer for a further 10 minutes, until reduced by a third. Strain the sauce through a wire sieve, pressing down on the lobster and prawn shells, and vegetables.

Pulse the lobster meat in a processor until finely minced. Take care not to overwork – you don't want a purée. Season with salt and pepper. Beat in whites of eggs and add as much of the cream as the mixture will take without becoming too liquid. Place the mixture in four ramekins (approximately 10cm to 12cm in diameter) and cover with tinfoil. Bake in a bain-marie for 15 minutes at 190° Celsius.

Spoon the sauce onto plates. Remove bavaroises from ramekins and place on top of the sauce. Garnish with dill or chives.

SYMPHONY OF SEAFOOD
Serves 2

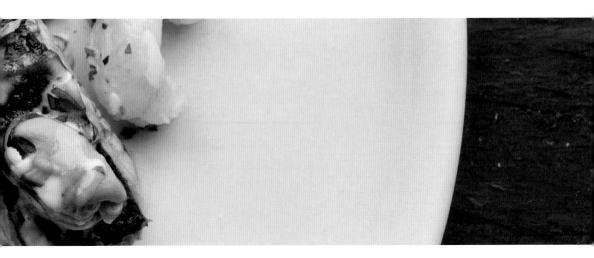

This was another classic dish in White's on the Green and also in Clifford's, in Cork and in Clonmel. Everything depends on the quality of the fish. There is no hiding place for second-rate produce in this dish. My dad did lots of variations on the sauce – one involved substituting sorrel for the watercress. Dad was very fond of sea urchins but they can be difficult and expensive to get, so feel free to leave them out.

—Peter Clifford

INGREDIENTS

1 fillet of sole, 150g to 200g
2 sea urchins, if available
4 Dublin Bay prawns
4 mussels
2 oysters
2 pieces of salmon,
    approximately 30g each
2 scallops

Sauce
1 shallot
1 knob of butter
125ml fish stock
125ml white wine
125ml cream
50g chopped watercress
10ml lemon juice
10mls olive oil

METHOD

Poach the sole, sea urchins, prawns, mussels and oysters. Lightly grill the salmon and scallops. Take care not to overcook the fish.

Chop the shallot and fry in olive oil. Add the fish stock and white wine and reduce by half. Add the cream and reduce by half again. Add the watercress, butter and lemon juice and season to taste.

To serve, spoon some sauce onto the plates, arrange seafood nicely on top and then add a final drizzle of sauce over the whole lot. *Bon appétit!*

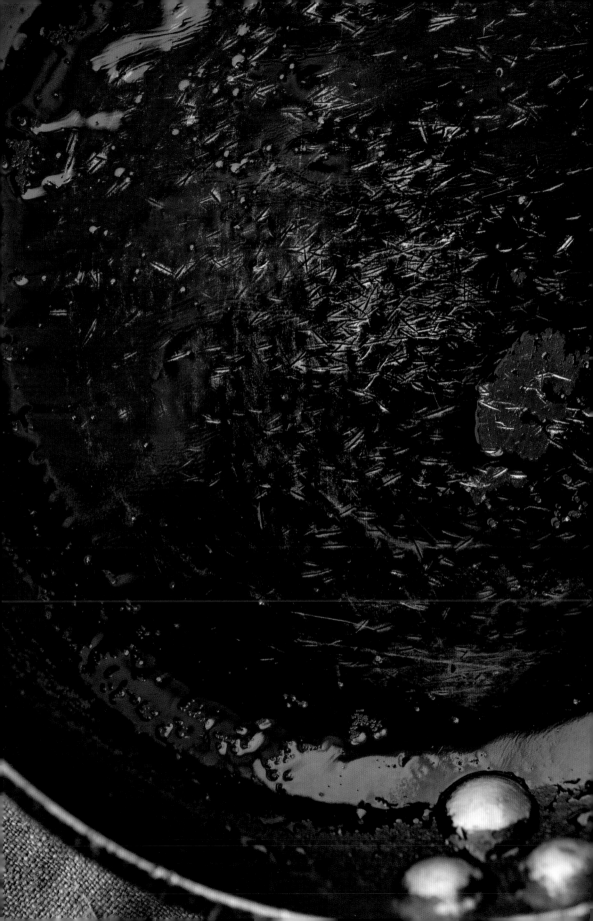

4

DESSERTS

GOAT CHEESE CAKE WITH RHUBARB, BLACK PEPPER AND ROSE VINEGAR JELLY

SERVES 6

It is crucial that the goat cheese is very young, soft, creamy and not too strong. A young Ardsallagh or Triskel would be excellent for this recipe. You probably won't be able to get rose vinegar in your local supermarket but it's simple to make. Just macerate a cupful of rose petals in as much white wine vinegar as it takes to cover them and a little splash extra. It's delicious and simple, but if I still can't persuade you to make it, try Mr Pettersen's Raspberry Vinegar, made down in west Cork. Apologies if the rhubarb sorbet isn't so simple. I admit it's a bit 'cheffy' and full of specialist ingredients, but that's the difference you sometimes taste when you eat out.

—Peter Clifford

INGREDIENTS

Goat Cheese Cake
7g to 8g gelatine
  (about 3 leaves)
500g soft goat cheese
125g sugar
100g ricotta
1 vanilla pod
320ml cream

Rose Vinegar Jelly
15g gelatine (about 6 leaves)
200ml rose vinegar or Mr
  Pettersen's Raspberry Vinegar

Rhubarb Sorbet
500g rhubarb, sliced
10g invert sugar
100g caster sugar
45g glucose
245ml water

Poached Rhubarb
6 rhubarb stalks, cut into
  5cm lengths
3l water
600g sugar
160ml red wine vinegar
50ml grenadine
3 star anise
2 vanilla pods
1 small bunch of mint

Black-Pepper Crumble
340g flour
280g sugar
180g soft butter
1 tsp freshly ground black
  pepper

METHOD

To make the cheesecake, soak the gelatine in cold water. Cream the goat cheese, ricotta, sugar and seeds from the vanilla pod in a food processor or by hand. Keeping back 20ml of the cream, whip the remaining 300ml into soft peaks. Gently heat the reserved 20ml of cream, remove from the heat, whisk in gelatine, leave to cool and mix into the goat-cheese mix. Then gently fold in the whipped cream. Place the mixture into a piping bag and leave to set in the fridge.

To make the rose vinegar jelly, soak gelatine in cold water, bring the rose vinegar to the boil in a saucepan, remove from the heat, allow to cool for a minute and then whisk in the gelatine. Put the mixture in the fridge. To make the rhubarb sorbet, cook the rhubarb in a pot with a splash of water (enough to just barely cover base of the pot) until soft, then purée. Place the invert sugar, caster sugar, glucose and water in a pot and bring to the boil. Remove from the heat, add the rhubarb purée and leave to cool. Freeze in an ice cream machine, or freeze in a container in the freezer for about 2 hours, mixing with a fork every 30 minutes.

To make the poached rhubarb, skin the rhubarb with a peeler and retain the skin. Bring the water, sugar, vinegar, grenadine, star anise, vanilla pods and mint to a boil. Pour the mixture onto rhubarb in a heatproof container deep enough to immerse it in syrup, and cover with cling film. When cool, place in a shallow container in the fridge. To make the black-pepper crumble, mix together the flour, sugar, butter and black pepper to get a sandy texture. Bake on a tray at 170° Celsius until a light-brown colour, about 15 to 20 minutes.

To serve, pipe the cheesecake onto a plate and garnish with jelly, sorbet and poached rhubarb. Sprinkle on the black-pepper crumble. (You can pipe as little or as much of the cheesecake mix as is desired, and it can also be put into a serving glass.)

LEMON-AND-BASIL SOUFFLÉ TART WITH WILD STRAWBERRIES

SERVES 6 TO 8

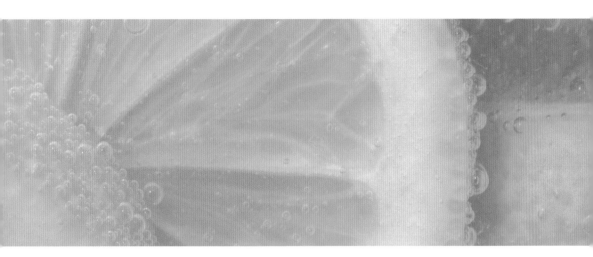

This is all about summer – fresh and light. I first did this in Ballyfin. They had the most amazing produce. We used to spin down to the gardens in golf buggies to get it.

—Peter Clifford

INGREDIENTS

Lemon-and-Basil Soufflé
280ml water
240g sugar
250g lemon juice
40g basil leaves
20g gelatine leaves

Pastry
250g butter, softened
250g icing sugar
3 small eggs
500g flour

Strawberries
1 bowl wild strawberries
    (approximately 200g)

METHOD

For the lemon-and-basil soufflé, make a syrup of water, sugar and lemon juice by bringing these ingredients to a low boil. Leave it to simmer for 7 minutes, without stirring after it begins to boil. Remove from the heat and put the basil in a pot to infuse for 30 minutes. After 20 minutes, put 20g gelatine to soak in cold water. When the gelatine is soft, squeeze out and whisk into syrup, which should still be warm. Pass through a sieve and place the bowl into a bowl of ice to set the jelly. Check after 1 hour – it should be wobbly.

When the jelly has just set, put into a standalone mixer with a whisk attachment and mix at full speed until it has risen to the top of the bowl and has volume. This will take about 30 minutes. Turn out into a shallow tray – approximately 5cm deep – lined with cling film. Put in the freezer for a couple of hours or until frozen.

For the pastry, cream the butter and icing sugar, then slowly add the eggs and the flour. Be careful not to overwork the pastry. Roll out the pastry to the thickness of a €1 coin. Place on a tray lined with greaseproof paper, then cover with another sheet of greaseproof paper and another tray, to keep the pastry flat while baking. Bake for 10 to 15 minutes in an oven preheated to 180° Celsius.

To serve, turn out the frozen lemon-and-basil soufflé and place on top of the pastry. Trim the edges and cut into serving-sized portions. Garnish with wild strawberries.

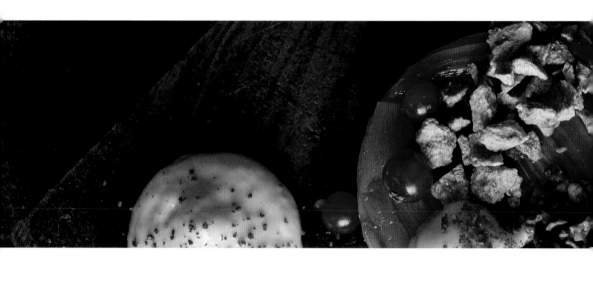

RHUBARB-AND-REDCURRANT TERRINE WITH GOAT CHEESE ICE CREAM

SERVES 6

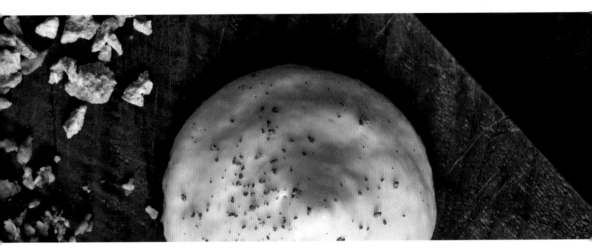

I came up with this dish in Pepper and it was probably the most popular dessert on the menu. Credit must go to my pastry chef, Marcela Santos, who had a lot of input into the design of this dish. In the restaurant, as you'll see from the picture, we garnish this dish with custard foam, granola and dehydrated rhubarb, but I think I've put you through enough for the moment and it's equally nice without those touches.

—Peter Clifford

INGREDIENTS

Terrine

7g to 8g gelatine
  (approximately 3 leaves)

300ml water

300g caster sugar

2 star anise

1 slice orange flesh, pith
  removed

1 cinnamon stick

100ml grenadine syrup

300g rhubarb, peeled and
  sliced into 3cm lengths

100g fresh redcurrants

Goat Cheese Ice Cream

500ml milk

250g fresh goat cream
  cheese

150g caster sugar

120g egg yolks

METHOD

To make the rhubarb and redcurrant terrine, first put the gelatine to soak in cold water. Place six metal rings, about 5cm deep and 10cm in diameter, on a flat tray and line with cling film, with the tray acting as the base. Place the water, sugar, star anise, orange and cinnamon in a pot, bring to a boil and simmer for 7 minutes, sieve and then add the grenadine. Reheat this mixture and use it to poach the rhubarb until it is tender but still holding its shape: 2 or 3 minutes at most. Carefully remove the rhubarb from the liquid and arrange the rhubarb and redcurrants in metal rings, as desired. Dissolve the gelatine in 300ml of the poaching syrup (if the syrup is cold, reheat gently but don't boil) and cover the rhubarb and redcurrants. Cover the moulds with cling film and leave to set in the fridge overnight.

To make the goat cheese ice cream, whisk the egg yolks and sugar until fluffy and pale. Heat the milk and, when just boiled, add it slowly to the egg-and-sugar mixture, whisking all the while. Pour the resulting liquid back into the pot and simmer over a low heat until it thickens. Remove from the heat. Mix in the crumbled goat cheese and stir in until completely incorporated. Place in an ice cream machine and follow the manufacturer's instructions, or place in a container in the freezer for 2 hours, mixing well with a fork every 30 minutes, then cover with cling film and leave to freeze.

To serve, turn out the terrine onto a plate and serve with a scoop of ice cream, some fresh redcurrants and a mint leaf.

RHUBARB CRUMBLE

Serves 4 to 6

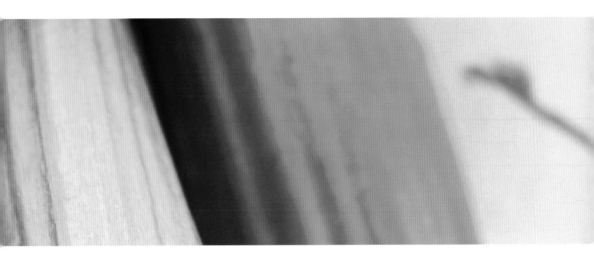

Just two ingredients for the fruit element and six simple ingredients for the topping – I think you'll find it fairly easy to tell that this was one of my dad's desserts and not one of mine?

—Peter Clifford

Ingredients

500g rhubarb
100g sugar
1 tbsp water
50g butter
50g wholemeal flour
50g oatmeal
50g brown sugar
25g mixed nuts, ground
1 tsp mixed spice

Method

Top and tail the rhubarb and cut it into 5cm lengths. Place the rhubarb and sugar into saucepan with 1 tbsp water and stew lightly on a low heat until the rhubarb is tender and the sugar has turned to syrup. Place the stewed rhubarb into one large ovenproof dish or individual ovenproof dishes.

Rub the butter into the flour and add the oatmeal, sugar, nuts and spices. Spread this topping evenly over the stewed rhubarb. Place in an oven preheated to 180° Celsius until the top is crisp and golden, about 15 minutes. Serve with vanilla ice cream, custard or some whipped cream.

APPLE TARTE TATIN WITH SPICED ICE CREAM AND RED-WINE FINANCIERS

Serves 6

This is another way of doing the classic tarte Tatin, a dessert that never, ever goes out of fashion. In the restaurant, we cook these in individual pastry shells that are about 10cm in diameter but, to make it easy for you and in case you don't have the shells, the recipe below is written using a single baking tray and the individual portions can be cut out afterwards.

—Peter Clifford

INGREDIENTS

Tart Tatin
6 sweet dessert apples
20g butter
180g sugar
20ml water
280g puff pastry

Spiced Ice Cream
500ml milk
1 star anise
10 cardamom pods, crushed
1 tsp ground nutmeg
1 tsp ground cinnamon
1 tsp ground cloves
1 tsp ground ginger
125g caster sugar
6 egg yolks (about 120g)

Financiers
175g melted butter
200g icing sugar
150g egg whites
135g ground almonds
55g plain flour

Red-Wine Syrup:
300ml red wine
150g sugar

METHOD

To make the tarte, set the oven to 180° Celsius and line a baking tray with parchment. Peel and core the apples, halve them and then cut each half into four wedges. Heat the butter and 100g of the sugar in a frying pan. When the sugar starts to caramelise, add the apples and cook until soft, about 4 to 5 minutes. Remove from the heat and allow to cool. Put 80g of sugar in a pot and add enough water to make a thick paste – about 20ml. Add it in stages, as you might not need it all. Put it on a medium heat and cook until sugar begins to turn into liquid caramel. Do not stir, or you will cause crystals to form. Pour the caramel onto a baking tray and cool for 2 to 3 minutes. Arrange the apples in a fan on the caramel. Prick the puff pastry with a fork and place over the apples. Tuck the pastry down at the edge of the tray, around the apples. Bake in a preheated oven at 180° Celsius for 15 minutes or until pastry is crisp and golden-brown. Allow to rest for 2 minutes and then place a tray the same size on top, and flip over so the caramelised apples are revealed.

To make the ice cream, put the milk and spices in a pot, bring to the boil, turn off, and allow to infuse for 30 minutes. Separately, whisk the sugar and yolks until pale. Pour the milk through a sieve over the egg yolks and sugar. Whisk together and put back into a pot on a low heat, stirring with a rubber spatula, until the mixture is thick enough to coat the back of a spoon. Strain and then freeze in an ice cream machine, or put in the freezer in a container for about 2 hours, whisking every 30 minutes.

To make the financiers, put the butter in a pan on a medium heat until just browning. Take off the heat and let cool slightly. Lightly mix the butter with the sugar, egg whites, almonds and flour. Put in a greased, greaseproof paper-lined baking tray and refrigerate for 30 minutes. Bake at 180° Celsius for 12 minutes or until golden-brown. To make the red-wine syrup, put the red wine and sugar in a pot and reduce (without stirring) at a low heat until syrupy, about 10 to 12 minutes.

To serve, slice the financiers into little cubes and soak them in the red-wine syrup for 2 to 3 minutes. Place the baked tarte Tatin on a serving plate and garnish it neatly with the financiers and a single quenelle of ice cream.

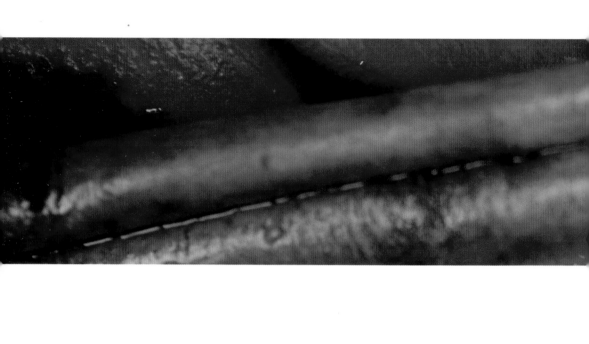

POACHED PLUMS IN RED WINE, SCENTED WITH CINNAMON AND GINGER

SERVES 4

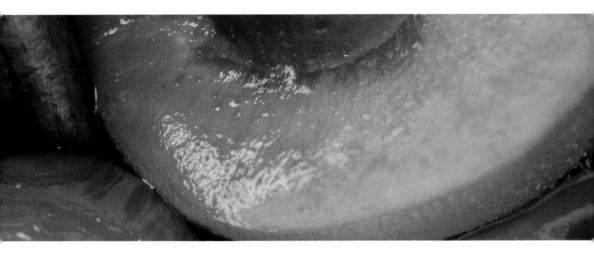

A really simple recipe, with the ginger and cinnamon adding spice. A lovely light dessert with vanilla ice cream, ideal to prepare beforehand for a dinner party. This would have been popular in Clifford's Bistro, in Cork, especially if you thought you had no room for a dessert.

—Peter Clifford

INGREDIENTS

300ml red wine

25g brown sugar

1 tbsp Irish honey

1 cinnamon stick, snapped in
half

1 tsp finely chopped root
ginger

Juice of 1 lemon

Juice of 1 orange

8 plums, halved, with stones
removed

METHOD

Combine all the ingredients except the plums and bring to a
low boil. Simmer for 7 to 10 minutes, until syrupy. Add the
plums and cook for 3 to 4 more minutes. Serve hot in a bowl
with some of the syrup drizzled over a scoop of ice cream.
If you prepare the spiced-wine syrup beforehand, you can
reheat just before serving and cook the plums to serve hot.

CARAMELISED CRÊPES FILLED WITH BANANAS
SERVES 8

This is a recipe from the bistro but my dad did it in Clonmel as well, and I've done it myself many times. It's like an '80s version of bannoffee pie. It is very popular with children of all ages and goes very well with a nice vanilla ice cream. It always just flew out the door.

—Peter Clifford

INGREDIENTS

Crêpes
150g flour
300ml milk
1 egg
50g butter

Caramel Sauce
250g sugar
150ml water
150ml cream
100g unsalted butter

Pastry Cream
250ml milk
2 to 3 drops of vanilla
  essence
3 egg yolks
50g caster sugar
50g plain flour
125ml whipped cream

Bananas
8 bananas, sliced

Garnish
Icing sugar, for dusting

METHOD

To make the crêpes, mix the flour, milk and egg. Melt the butter and then whisk it into the milk mixture. Let the mixture rest in the fridge for 1 hour, then grease and heat a heavy pan and cook 8 crepes: ladle in crêpe mixture and swirl the pan to cover the entire base; when air bubbles pop up, flip and finish.

To make the caramel sauce, boil the sugar and water in a saucepan until the sugar is dissolved. Allow to caramelise until nut brown in colour. Remove from the heat and whisk in cream and butter. Be very careful of 'spitting' hot liquid as you add the cream and butter. Set aside for later use.

To make the pastry cream, boil the milk and add the vanilla. Set aside. Cream the egg yolks and sugar, add the flour and mix well. Add a little of the milk and continue to mix. Then pour in remaining milk. Return to the heat and cook until the mix is coming away from the side of the pot and gathering in the centre. Allow to cool.

Warm the crêpes and place them flat on plates. Reheat the caramel sauce, add the sliced bananas to the pot and remove from the heat. Fold in the whipped cream to the pastry cream. Place a spoonful of pastry cream in the centre of each crêpe. Pour the caramel-and-banana mixture neatly around the crepes. Fold the crêpes. Dust with icing sugar.

CHOCOLATE MARQUISE

Serves 10 to 12

This is one of dad's recipes that he picked up on a *stage* in France. It was very popular in Clifford's and he used to serve it with coulis, which was only really coming into Ireland around that time. A must for the chocaholic.

—Peter Clifford

Ingredients

250g chocolate (at least 65 to 75 percent)

100g caster sugar

175g butter, diced and softened

5 egg whites

Pinch of salt

5 egg yolks

Method

Melt the chocolate in a double boiler or a bowl over a pot of water. Add the sugar and beat with a fork. Beat in the butter, piece by piece. Meanwhile, separately, whisk the egg whites and salt until very stiff. Then whisk the egg yolks, one at a time, into the chocolate mix. Remove the top of the double boiler from the heat and carefully fold the stiff egg whites into the chocolate mixture. Fill a cling-film-lined loaf tin with the mixture. Leave in the freezer for 12 hours. Remove from the freezer, slice, garnish with seasonal berries and mint, and serve.

CHOCOLATE CRÉMEUX WITH RASPBERRY PARFAIT AND DOUGHNUTS

Serves 8

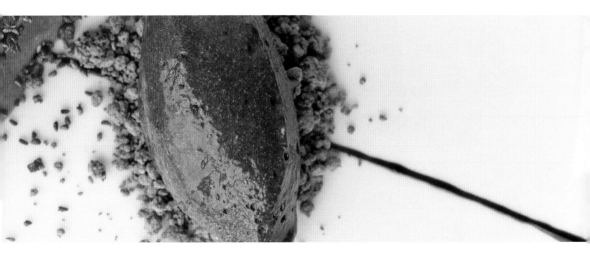

I've developed a bit of an obsession with doughnuts. They can seem a bit fiddly but nothing you buy in a shop will ever compare to the taste of a just-cooked doughnut – worth all the trouble every time, in my opinion.

—Peter Clifford

Ingredients

Parfait
300g raspberries, puréed
6 large eggs
2 large yolks
100g sugar

Chocolate Crémeux
250ml milk
250ml cream
50g sugar
100g egg yolks
200g dark chocolate,
  chopped
125g unsalted butter, cubed

Doughnut Starter
12g fresh yeast
125ml water
225g strong flour

Doughnut Dough
12g fresh yeast
60ml milk
6 egg yolks
60g butter
510g strong flour
90g sugar
10g salt

Garnish
Granulated sugar

Method

For the parfait, blend the raspberries and pass through sieve. Place the raspberry purée, eggs, egg yolks and sugar in a bowl. Put the bowl over a pot of simmering water without letting its bottom touch the water. Keep whisking and cooking until the mixture thickens and reduces slightly. Remove from the heat and place over a container of ice water to stop the cooking. Pour into a mould (a single terrine mould or individual ramekins) lined with cling film, and freeze overnight.

For the chocolate crémeux, heat the milk and cream in a pot. Meanwhile, whisk the sugar and egg yolks in a bowl until fluffy and pale. Pour the milk and cream slowly over the yolk-and-sugar mix, whisking constantly. Pour the resulting mixture back into the pot and simmer, stirring with a rubber spatula to keep from curdling. Take it off the heat when it thickens enough to coat the back of a spoon. While the mixture is still warm enough, add chocolate to melt into it, stirring gently. Cool at room temperature for about an hour. Put the resulting chocolate custard in a blender and add butter gradually until fully incorporated. Refrigerate.

To make the doughnuts, first make the starter. Dissolve the yeast in the water, add the flour and bring together until a dough is formed. Knead until elastic. Let prove at room temperature until doubled in size. To make the doughnut dough, dissolve the yeast in milk and then add the egg yolks and butter. Separately, mix the flour, sugar and salt. Add this to the yeast mixture and the risen starter. Knead until smooth and elastic. Prove this dough at room temperature until it begins to rise again but has not yet doubled. Knock it back down, roll it out with a pin until it is 1cm thick and cut out desired shapes and sizes. You can experiment with balls and squares, but cut out circles with large cookie cutters and cut smaller circles within those to achieve classic doughnut shapes.

Let the doughnuts prove at room temperature for an hour. Deep-fry at 160° Celsius, turning regularly to cook both sides. Roll in granulated sugar while still warm. To serve, arrange on each plate a slice of parfait, a spoon or even a quenelle of crémeux, and one large doughnut or several smaller doughnut shapes.

CHOCOLATE FONDANT WITH GUINNESS ICE CREAM
SERVES 8

I do these all the time, they're the first thing you do in college, but this one is quite different – it uses ground almonds and rice flour. The ice cream is a bit unusual as well, in that it uses brown sugar, and it is quite Irish as well. The flavour goes very well with the fondant.

—Peter Clifford

INGREDIENTS

Fondant

250g dark chocolate (at least
  70 percent)
110g unsalted butter
85g rice flour
85g ground almonds
4 whole eggs
85g caster sugar
Cocoa powder for dusting

Guinness Ice Cream

300ml Guinness, just-opened
300ml cream
15g glucose syrup
150g egg yolks
80g brown sugar

METHOD

Butter eight moulds or ramekins (about 10cm in diameter) and set aside. Melt the chocolate and butter to 35° Celsius in a double boiler or a bowl over a pot of simmering water. Mix the rice flour and almonds in a separate bowl. Using a hand mixer, whisk the egg whites in a third bowl, adding the sugar slowly until the whites have a nice shine and form stiff peaks. Add the egg yolks to the chocolate-and-butter mixture and gently fold in the rice-flour-and-almond mixture. Fold in the egg whites very gently in three stages, using an equal portion of egg whites each time. Lightly dust moulds or ramekins with cocoa powder and then spoon the fondant mixture into them. Tap the moulds gently on your work surface to allow the mixture to set evenly. Let chill in the fridge for at least 3 hours.

To make the ice cream, put the Guinness, cream and glucose syrup in a pot, bring to a simmer and then remove from the heat. Separately, whisk the egg yolks and sugar together until very pale. Pour the Guinness-and-cream mixture into the sugar-and-yolk mixture, whisking all the time. Then pour the result into a clean pot and cook on a gentle heat until it reaches 70° Celsius. This will take approximately 5 minutes. Cool this mixture and finish in an ice cream machine until frozen, or put in a container in the freezer and whisk every 2 hours until frozen and creamy. (This takes longer to set than some of the other recipes because of the Guinness.)

To serve, heat the oven to 180° Celsius and bake fondant in the moulds on a baking tray for 10 minutes. Remove from oven and allow to cool for 1 minute. Unmould the fondant onto a serving plate and put a spoonful of ice cream alongside. In the restaurant we serve this with a roasted cocoa-nib tuile, but it's just as nice without!

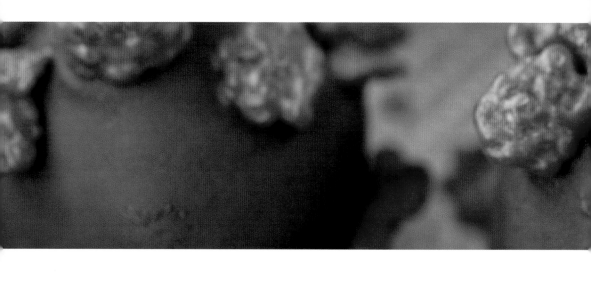

WHITE CHOCOLATE AND DRIED CRANBERRY TRUFFLES

MAKES 30+ TRUFFLES

This is a little *petit four* recipe. I change them every week, so I'm constantly coming up with new ones. If you're not very experienced at working with chocolate, this isn't too difficult, but you will find it much easier if you have a thermometer to gauge the heat of the chocolate.

—Peter Clifford

INGREDIENTS

500g white chocolate,
  chopped

250ml cream

150g unsalted butter, room
  temperature

250g dried cranberries,
  chopped

200g dark chocolate,
  chopped

METHOD

Place the white chocolate in a bowl. Heat the cream until just boiled, take off the heat, pour over the white chocolate and mix until melted. Whisk in the butter until it's melted and the mixture takes on a glossy sheen, then add cranberries. Refrigerate the mixture for about 2.5 hours until completely set, then shape into balls the size of normal truffles, by hand or using a melon scoop.

Heat the dark chocolate in a double boiler to 35° Celsius. Using a fork, dip the white-chocolate-and-cranberry balls into the melted dark chocolate and then place them on a tray lined with parchment paper. Just balance the chocolate balls on the fork when you're doing this – don't stab them with it! If the dark chocolate is any hotter than 35° Celsius, it might melt the chocolate balls and the dark chocolate coating will definitely be too thin. Before the dark chocolate coating is set, sprinkles can be used or the truffles can be rolled in cocoa powder.

WHITE-CHOCOLATE GANACHE WITH RASPBERRY-AND-PROSECCO SORBET

SERVES 8

Probably the most popular dessert we ever put on in Pepper and, without doubt, the best white-chocolate ganache I've ever come up with. I did it for Taste of Dublin as well and it was crazy popular. I remember someone coming into the restaurant and ordering it – and then ordering another portion immediately after she had finished the first! And it's a really simple dessert.

—Peter Clifford

Ingredients

Ganache
4g gelatine (about 1.5 leaves)
300ml cream
50ml water
12g glucose syrup
1.5g agar-agar
250g white chocolate, melted

Sorbet
120ml water
80g caster sugar
500g raspberry purée
Juice of 1 lemon
500ml Prosecco, just-opened

Method

To make the ganache, start by soaking the gelatine leaves in cold water and lining an approximately 4cm-deep kitchen tray with cling film. Place the cream, water and glucose in a pot and bring gently to the boil. Add the agar-agar, whisking constantly, and boil for at least 2 minutes. Squeeze out the gelatine to remove excess water and then whisk into the cream mixture until fully dissolved. Pour the cream mixture into the already melted chocolate, whisking until fully incorporated. Pour the result into the lined tray, let it cool for 30 minutes at room temperature and then refrigerate for 4 hours or until set.

To make the sorbet, bring the water and sugar to a gentle boil for 7 minutes to create a syrup. Let cool, mix with the raspberry purée and lemon juice in a bowl, and stir with a wooden spoon, slowly adding the Prosecco. (It is important not to add the Prosecco while the mixture is still hot.) Chill this mixture and place in an ice cream machine until frozen. Otherwise, place in the freezer for about 2 hours, whisking it every half hour until frozen.

To serve, slice the ganache to the desired portion size, place on a plate and garnish with a quenelle of the sorbet. If it seems easier, the ganache can be made in individual serving glasses and the sorbet served on top.

CARAMEL CAKE WITH BITTER-CHOCOLATE SORBET, POACHED PEARS AND POPCORN

SERVES 8

I think my dad would have completely freaked out if someone had served him a plate with popcorn on it, in any shape or form, but then he knew that I was especially keen on desserts and the places and experiments they've led me to, so I guess he would have at least tried it.

—Peter Clifford

INGREDIENTS

Sponge for Caramel Cake
75g butter, softened
200g sugar
3 eggs
250g plain flour
1 tsp baking powder
1 tsp bread soda

Caramel Syrup
160g sugar
175ml water
3 cardamom pods,
  bashed but whole
30g butter

Bitter-Chocolate Sorbet
200ml milk
300ml water
75g caster sugar
50g glucose
300g dark chocolate,
  chopped

Poached Pears
150ml water
150g caster sugar
4 pears

Popcorn
50g popcorn kernels
150g brown sugar
1 pinch cinnamon

METHOD

To make the sponge for the caramel cake, preheat the oven to 180° Celsius. Beat the butter and sugar together. Add the eggs one by one and keep on beating until you have a smooth, fluffy mixture. Sieve in the flour, baking powder and baking soda, then fold these ingredients in gently and bake in a tray for 25 to 30 minutes.

To make the caramel syrup, place the sugar and 15ml of the water in a pot and put over a medium heat. In a separate pot, bring 160ml of water and the cardamom pods to the boil. In the caramel syrup pot, when the sugar starts to caramelise and change its colour to a deep golden brown – watch carefully, this will happen all of a sudden, so don't leave the pot unattended – add the butter, whisking slowly and carefully. Pour the cardamom water through sieve to remove the pods, then add the infused water to the caramel. Be very careful doing this, as it is likely to spit and splash very hot liquid! Bring it back to the boil and then remove from the heat.

To make the bitter-chocolate sorbet, boil the milk, water, sugar and glucose in a pot. When it comes to a boil, take off the heat and add the chocolate. After the chocolate has completely melted, bring the mixture to a boil again and then remove from the heat. Pass the mixture through a sieve. Pour the strained mixture into an ice cream machine and follow the manufacturer's instructions, or freeze the mixture in a container for 2 hours, mixing with a fork every 30 minutes.

To make the poached pears, bring the water and sugar to the boil and keep at a simmering boil for 7 minutes to make a light syrup. Peel the pears, remove the pips and cut the fruit lengthways. (In the picture for this dish, I have used a melon baller to achieve a very pleasing shape, but cutting into quarters is fine.) Place the pears in the syrup and poach over a low-to-medium heat until tender. Remove from heat and set aside.

For the popcorn, if you're feeling lazy, you could start with a bag of ready-made popcorn. Otherwise, heat a large saucepan, add the kernels and keep the pan covered until the popping sound more or less stops. Melt the sugar with cinnamon in another pot. Drizzle over the popcorn and stir.

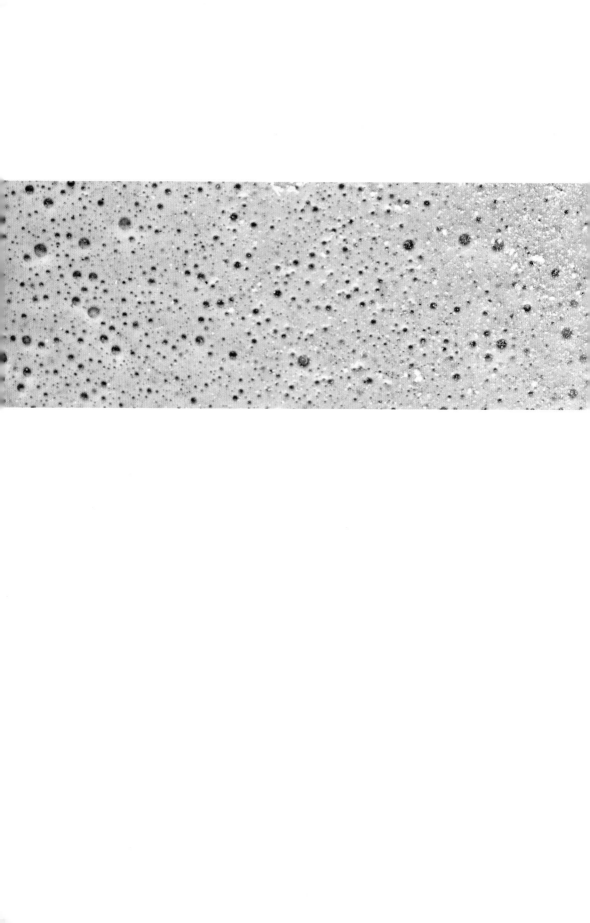

PISTACHIO MARSHMALLOWS
MAKES 25 TO 30

A lovely *petit four* with afternoon tea or coffee. The pistachio gives a wonderful, light nutty taste to complement the airy sweetness of the marshmallow. If you can't buy pistachio paste, it is quite easy to make your own with unsalted pistachios. Simply blend them with a splash of water, 1 tsp icing sugar and a knob of butter.

—Peter Clifford

INGREDIENTS

10g gelatine (about 4 leaves)
50g egg whites
250g caster sugar
50ml water
1 tbsp glucose
1 tbsp pistachio paste
Icing sugar to dust

METHOD

First, line a shallow baking tray with parchment paper, to put the marshmallow in to set. Put the gelatine leaves in cold water to soak. Separately, using an electric mixer, lightly whisk the egg whites until they are just forming peaks. Place the sugar, water and glucose in a pot and boil until syrup reaches 120° Celsius. Pour the syrup into the egg whites and whisk until fully incorporated. Squeeze out the gelatine leaves and whisk into the syrup-and-egg-white mix. Then whisk in the pistachio paste. Transfer the mixture to the prepared container, cover tightly with cling film and let set at room temperature for approximately 45 minutes. Cut into cubes and sprinkle with icing sugar. Store in an airtight container.

Note: You will need a sugar thermometer for this recipe.